EVERYDAY THINGS IN ARCHAIC GREECE

FIG. 1.—The Warrior's Departure.

(*From a Corinthian Krater, Pl. xxxiii., Buschor.*)

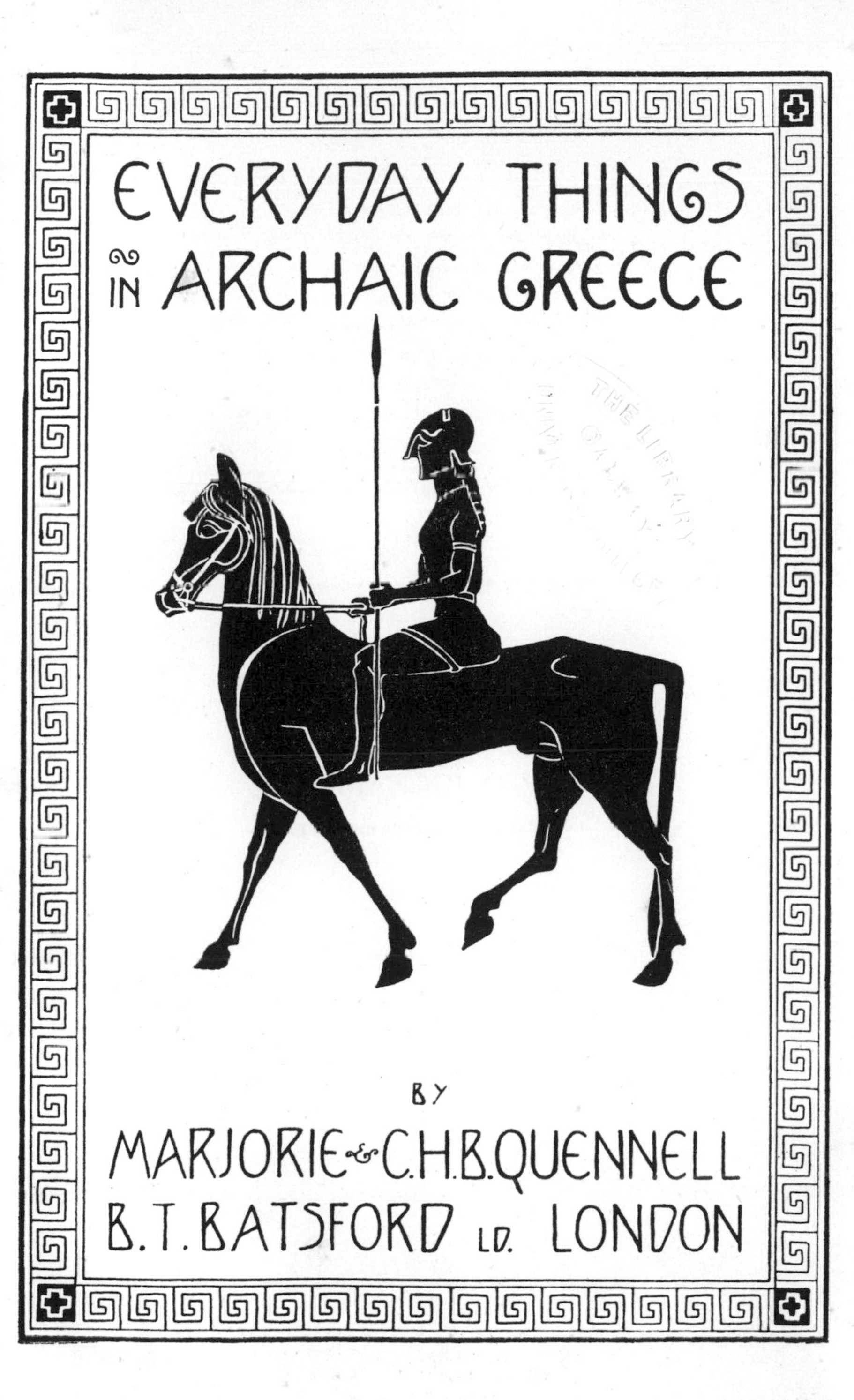
EVERYDAY THINGS
IN ARCHAIC GREECE
BY
MARJORIE & C.H.B. QUENNELL
B.T. BATSFORD LD. LONDON

TO THE READER

Since, therefore, few men are thus gifted, and yet it is required of the architect to be generally well-informed, and it is manifest he cannot hope to excel in each art, we beseech those who read this our work to pardon and overlook grammatical errors ; for we write and draw neither as accomplished philosophers, eloquent rhetoricians, nor expert grammarians, but as an architect and painter : in respect, however, of our art and its principles, we lay down rules which may serve as an authority to those who build, as well as to those who are already somewhat acquainted with the science.

A paraphrase from the end of the first chapter of Vitruvius' "Architecture."

TO RICHARD

A Great Brick-builder

First Edition, Spring 1931

MADE AND PRINTED IN GREAT BRITAIN
FOR THE PUBLISHERS, B. T. BATSFORD LTD.
BY THE DARIEN PRESS, EDINBURGH

PREFACE

THIS book, on the Archaic Period, is the second of the three on Greece which we are writing for boys and girls. It deals with a time which is of the greatest interest and the utmost importance to all of us who live now in Western Europe and America. It was not only our fate which was settled between 560 and 480 B.C., but the mode of our lives, the colour of our thoughts, and the fashion of our buildings. It may not be a vain imagining to wonder what would have happened to us if the Persians had won the battle of Salamis. Had their thrust been more successful than that tremendous wave of Mohammedan invasion which was not stopped until it reached Poitiers in 732 A.D., there might have been a greater struggle than that between the Cross and the Crescent.

If we turn from the political significance of the Greek struggle with the Persians to their technical accomplishments, we have a rich mine in which to quarry. During the Archaic Period, the details of the Doric style of architecture were finally fixed. The temples at Ægina and Pæstum led the way to the Parthenon. The Ionic experiments at Ephesus made the Erectheum possible. In sculpture the sculptors cut almost everything that can be carved in stone and marble, without losing architectural significance. The black-figure vases are exquisite, and the subjects of their decorations as illuminating as historical documents.

To-day, when trade is bad, and we find considerable difficulty in selling the massed produced oddments of a "Gadjet" Age, we might take a leaf out of the Greek book and try our hand at making beautiful things.

MARJORIE AND C. H. B. QUENNELL.

BERKHAMSTEAD, HERTS.,
May 1931.

CHART

Kings.	Current Events.	Literature.	Science.	Art.
		Solon, 639-559		c. 620. Heræum-Olympia
			624-546. Thales of Miletus	590. Temple of Apollo-Syracuse
				580. Olympieum-Syracuse
Crœsus, King of Lydia, 560	Ionian Greek cities reduced to dependence by Crœsus		566. Glaucus of Chios invents iron welding	570. Selinus 550. Selinus
553	Cyrus revolts against Astyages			
550	Cyrus overthrows the Medes	Æsopus (Fables) at Court of Crœsus	551. Anaximander of Miletus, Geographer	Harpy Tomb from Xanthos, Lycia, Asia Minor
547	Cyrus conquers Lydia			
545	Cyrus conquers Ionian cities		540. Anaximenes of Miletus	
				c. 540. Temple at Selinus
544	Phocæans leave Ionia			c. 540. Temple at Pæstum
538	Cyrus takes Babylon		572-497. Pythagoras of Samos	c. 540. Temple at Corinth
529	Cambyses succeeds Cyrus on Persian throne			c. 530. Temple at Selinus
525	Persians conquer Egypt	Æschylus born		c. 527. Temple at Athens
522	Death of Cambyses			520. Temple at Pæstum
521	Darius becomes King of Persia			
520	Cleomenes, King of Sparta			
517	Persians conquer Barca	518. Birth of Pindar		515. Athenian Treasury, Delphi
514	Scythian expedition of Darius			510. Acragas-Heracles
507	Cleomenes at Athens			
499	Failure of Naxian expedition			
498	Sardis burnt	496. Birth of Sophocles		
493	Persians take Chios, Lesbos, Tenedos	Phrynichus fined		
	Themistocles fortifies the Peiræus			
	Expedition of Mardonius			
491	Persians defeated at Marathon			489. Ægina-Aphæa
487	Egypt revolts			485. Syracuse-Athena
485	Death of Darius	484. Birth of Herodotus		
480	Salamis	Birth of Euripides		
479	Battle of Platæa			

CONTENTS

RECOMMENDED BOOKS

Title	Author / Edition	Publisher
HERODOTUS . . .	Canon Rawlinson's translation	John Murray, 1875
Or two volumes in the Everyman Edition		J. M. Dent & Sons
PAUSANIAS' DESCRIPTION OF GREECE	J. G. Frazer	Macmillan, 1898
ATLAS OF ANCIENT AND CLASSICAL GEOGRAPHY	Everyman Edition	J. M. Dent & Sons
SMALL CLASSICAL ATLAS		John Murray
SMALLER CLASSICAL DICTIONARY	Everyman Edition	J. M. Dent & Sons
THE ARCHITECTURE OF ANCIENT GREECE	Anderson, Spiers, and Dinsmoor	Batsford, 1927
GREEK AND ROMAN ARCHITECTURE	D. S. Robertson	Camb. Univ. Press, 1929
THE ARCHITECTURE OF MARCUS VITRUVIUS POLLIO		Lockwood & Co., 1874
A COMPANION TO GREEK STUDIES	Ed. by Leonard Whibley	Camb. Univ. Press, 1916
GUIDE TO DEPARTMENT OF GREEK AND ROMAN ANTIQUITIES IN THE BRITISH MUSEUM		Trustees of the British Museum
GUIDE TO DEPARTMENT OF GREEK AND ROMAN LIFE		Trustees of the British Museum
HANDBOOK OF THE CLASSICAL COLLECTIONS	Metropolitan MSS.	New York, Richter, 1927
THE DAILY LIFE OF THE GREEKS AND ROMANS	Metropolitan MSS.	New York, M'Clees, 1928
ANCIENT FURNITURE . .	Gisela M. A. Richter.	Clarendon Press, 1926
GREEK VASE PAINTING .	Ernst Buschor	Chatto & Windus, 1921
ALTKRETA . . .	Helmuth Th. Bossert-	Ernst Wasmuth, A.-G., Berlin, 1923
CHAPTERS ON GREEK DRESS	Maria Millington Evans	Macmillan, 1893
THE CRŒSUS TEMPLE OF ARTEMIS	Henderson	Journal R.I.B.A., 5th December 1908

EVERYDAY THINGS IN ARCHAIC GREECE

CHAPTER I.—HERODOTUS AND HIS HISTORY

In Volume I., "Homeric Greece," we told of the wonderful Mycenæan civilisation which was built up on the mainland of Greece, after the overthrow of the Minoans at Cnossos, in the island of Crete. We illustrated the former by the excavations of Schliemann at Tiryns, and the latter by the discoveries of Sir Arthur Evans, and we attempted to give the whole some unity, by linking it up with the tales of the Argonauts, the "Iliad" and the "Odyssey." We did this because, to the Greeks of the Classical Period of the fifth century B.C., Homer was regarded not only as a poet but a historian of the heroic doings of their own forefathers in a Golden Age.

The date of the Golden Age of the Trojan War was about 1192-1183 B.C., and here we wish to trace what happened between this time and the battle of Salamis in 480 B.C., when the Greeks defeated the Persians. This battle was very important, because it marked the beginning of the great Classical Period in Greece.

To go back to the days after the Trojan War then, Agamemnon and his men returned to Mycenæ, and Odysseus to Penelope in Ithaca. About 1100 B.C. there appear to have been disturbances in Thessaly and the regions to the north of Greece. Perhaps news reached the people there of the wealth of Mycenæ. These newcomers were the Dorians, and they descended on Mycenæan Greece from the North, in much the same way as our own Anglo-Saxons did on Roman Britain, and being a rough and rude people were quite unable to maintain the Mycenæan civilisation.

So a dark age descended on Greece, and the original inhabitants fled across the Ægean Sea to Asia Minor, where they settled in Æolia and Ionia (see Fig. 2).

They went as fugitives, and Herodotus tells us that those who came from Athens, and considered themselves the purest Ionians, did not, or could not, take their wives with them, but married and carried off Carian girls, after having killed their fathers. For this reason, the wives bound themselves by oath " that none should ever sit at meat with her husband, or call him by his name." Not a very good start for matrimony.

The next important date is about the tenth or ninth century B.C., when Homer was writing his poems, and not only laying the foundations of Literature in Western Europe, but inspiring the scattered Greeks to rise again. It is probable that Homer himself was an Ionian, and wrote for his fellow-countrymen of the glorious life led by their forefathers in the homeland of Greece before their flight.

Without this knowledge of a glorious past, and the feeling that they were descended from heroes, they could not have emerged from the darkness of the age which followed the overthrow of the Mycenæan civilisation, or have steeled themselves to meet the Persians at Salamis and defeat them, nor would they have been able to build once more another and yet more glorious civilisation in the age of Pericles.

By the eighth century B.C. the Greek colonies in Asia Minor were so well established that Ephesus, Miletus, Smyrna, and Phocæa were great cities.

After a while the Dorians who had settled in Greece began to send out emigrants. The small Greek city State was rather like a beehive. When its population increased, and food supplies began to fail, a swarm was sent out to find a new home. They were a seafaring

Fig. 2.—Map of Greece and Her Colonies.

people, like our own Vikings, so they took their ships and sailed away to the islands and coastlands of the Mediterranean and the Black Sea, and settled down and founded colonies in the Cyclades, Corcyra (Corfu), and Crete, in Sicily and South Italy, and many other places. In their travels they learned much from the still older civilisations of the Near East.

Then some of them returned to Greece. The father of Hesiod, the poet who was thought worthy to rank with Homer, came from Æolia in Asia Minor and settled in Bœotia. Hesiod, probably as early as the eighth century B.C., wrote his "Theogony," which gave Greek religion its form, and regularised their ideas of the gods and goddesses.

By 776 the Greeks of the homeland and the colonies had so far come together that they were able to hold a great festival at Olympia, and of what this meant we shall write later.

The stage is now set for the introduction of one of the first great characters in Greek History, Herodotus of Halicarnassus, in Caria, Asia Minor, born about 484 B.C., the father and first of all the historians. Like many Greeks, he was forced to fly from his own city, and set out on travels which led him to the island of Samos, to Egypt, and then, in the time of Pericles, to Athens. He was writing his history as late as 428, and died about 425 B.C. As an Ionian he was well qualified to write of the Greek colonies. He explains an Ionian as one who came from Athens and kept the Apaturia (an annual meeting of the Phratries for registering the birth of children entitled to citizenship).

He tells how, when the emigrants left Greece, they took fire from the sacred hearth to the new settlement, where it was kept always alight in the Prytaneum or Government House; it symbolised the life of the State.

So Herodotus tells us of these city States, and contrasts

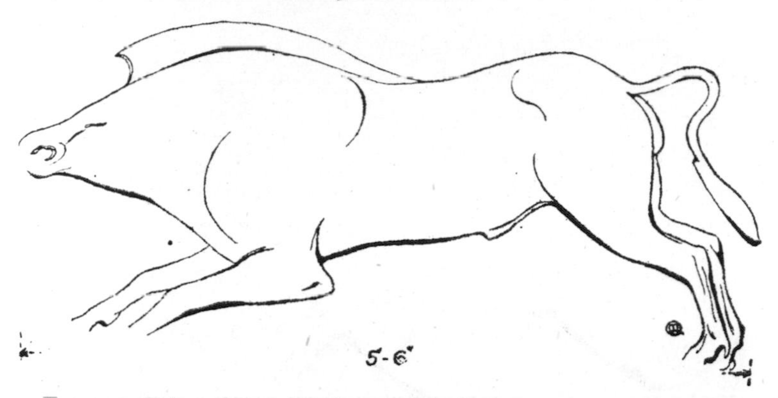

FIG. 3. Frieze from the Acropolis, Xanthos, about 500 B.C.
(*British Museum.*)

them with the powers of Egypt, Assyria, and Persia, which waxed and waned as neighbours.

The unity and dramatic quality of his work comes from this conflict between the puny Greek States and the might of Persia. It is the story of David and Goliath, with a David left wondering at the end whether the giant can really be dead. We are interested in the tale, because, if the Greeks had not defeated the Persians at Salamis, we in Western Europe would not be leading the lives we are to-day; Classical Greece would not have come into being, or our opportunity to inherit, through Rome, some part of her knowledge.

The joy in the work of Herodotus comes from the fact that he painted his picture on a big canvas, and used many colours. He gives us everything, gossip, legend, and history. He tells us quite frankly that he cannot be sure that all are true, but even with this qualification we feel that it is good to know what was the current gossip of the time, and his book is as alive as a newspaper of to-day.

Herodotus opens with a reference to the Trojan War, and cites this as a cause of the enmity between the Greeks and Persians.

He divided his history into nine books, or chapters.

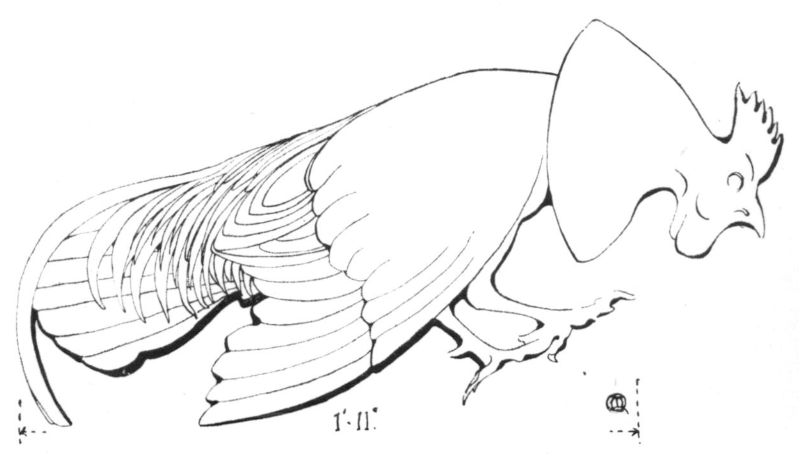

Fig. 4.—Part of Frieze from Xanthos.

In the *FIRST BOOK* we read how Crœsus, King of Lydia, first conquered the Æolians, Ionians, and Dorians of Asia Minor in 560 B.C. Before his time they had been free, probably because their settlements were not considered to be of much importance. This was the beginning of the long fight which was to terminate at Salamis, after eighty years of crowded history. Ephesus was the first city attacked by Crœsus, and he finally conquered nearly all Asia Minor. Solon, the Athenian, visited his Court at Sardis.

Then, hearing that the Persians under Cyrus were becoming very powerful, he determined to consult various oracles, including the one at Delphi. This is very extraordinary—that Crœsus, who was not a Greek, should have sent to the great shrine in Greece, situated in Phocis, to the north of the Gulf of Corinth. The advice of the Delphic oracle, or Crœsus' interpretation of it, was so disastrous that it would have been better for him if he had refrained. Their first answer was to a test question devised by Crœsus, and was so satisfactory that he sacrificed to the Delphic gods, and gathered together a great store of golden ingots, the statue of a lion in gold, and another of

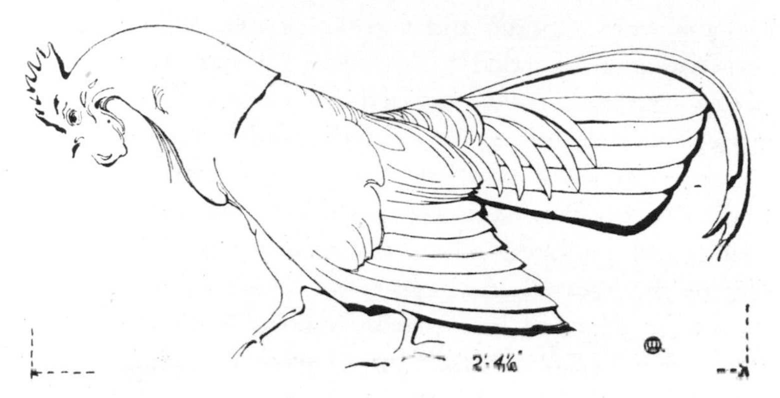

FIG. 5.—Archaic Frieze, Acropolis, Xanthos.
(*British Museum.*)

a woman, bowls of gold and silver, four silver casks, lustral vases, and the necklaces and girdles of his wife. Gold was found in Lydia. All this treasure was sent to Delphi, and the oracles again consulted as to his chance of success if he went to war against the Persians. The oracles replied to this, that if Crœsus attacked the Persians he would destroy a mighty empire, but that he must make alliance with the most powerful of the Greeks. Another answer seemed just as satisfactory, so Crœsus proposed an alliance with the Spartans. They replied that they were willing to help, and sent him a bronze vase, which unfortunately went astray. Meanwhile Crœsus invaded Cappadocia, hoping to defeat Cyrus.

A Lydian wise man warned him against warring with men who wore leathern clothes and trousers; whose country was sterile; who drank water, not wine; who had no figs, or anything nice to eat; and who, if they once realised how pleasant life was in Lydia, would never be content until they conquered the country. At this time the Persians had not been enervated by the luxury which surprised the Greeks after the battle of Platæa (p. 30).

No decision was reached in the first encounter. The Lydians were a brave and warlike people, who fought on horseback, and carried long lances. Cyrus thought of a clever stratagem, and opposed his camels to the Lydian horses, because horses hate camels, and cannot bear either the sight or smell of them. When the battle began, the Lydian war-horses, seeing and smelling the camels, turned round and galloped off, and Crœsus was defeated. He sent to the Spartans for help; but, as generally happened, they were engaged in a private quarrel with the Argives. This quarrel resolved itself into a trial by combat between 300 from each side, who fought till only two Argives and one Spartan remained. The armies then took up the quarrel, and in the end the Spartans gained the victory. Upon this the Argives, who had worn their hair long, cut it off short, and the Spartans passed a law that henceforward they should wear theirs long, though before they had always cut it short. So no help was sent to Crœsus, and the walled city of Sardis was taken after a fourteen days' siege. He fulfilled the Delphic oracle by destroying not the Persian but his own empire (547 B.C.).

After a while, Crœsus was treated kindly by Cyrus, and when his fetters were struck off, he sent these to Delphi. The pythoness replied that he should have sent to Delphi again, to find out which empire would be destroyed, so he had only himself to blame. The pythoness was the medium between the god and the priests.

Herodotus then tells us of all that the Lydians had done, how the tomb of Alyattes, the father of Crœsus, was formed with a base of immense blocks of stone (the sepulchral chamber), the rest being a vast mound of earth with five stone pillars at the top. It was Alyattes who sent, as an offering to Delphi, a curiously inlaid steel salver made by Glaucus the Chian, who first invented the inlaying of steel.

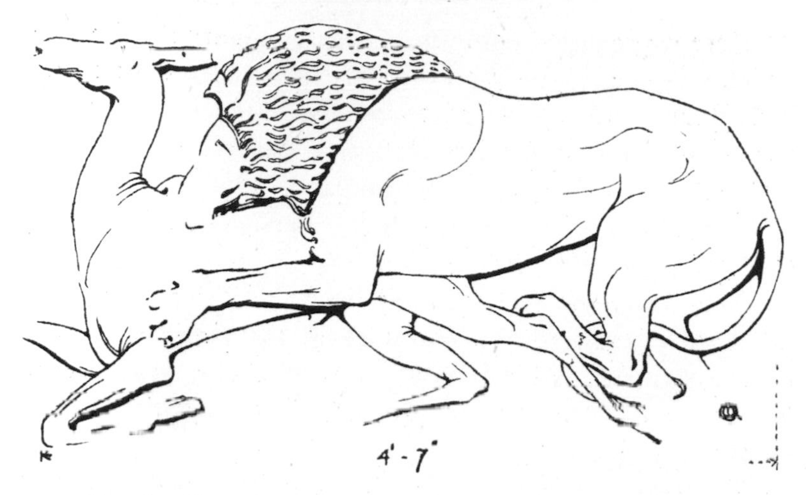

FIG. 6.—Part of a Fricze from the Acropolis at Xanthos.
(*British Museum.*)

He tells us as well how the Lydians were the first people to use gold and silver coins, and to sell goods by retail. They claimed also the invention of games, which were common with the Greeks. It came about in this way: there was once a famine through the whole of Lydia, which they bore patiently, but finding that it did not pass away, they set to work to devise remedies for the evil. Various persons invented the games of dice, knuckle-bones, and ball, but not tables. Then they all played games one day so vigorously that they did not feel hungry, and the next day they ate what was going, but did not play. In this way eighteen years passed.

Herodotus next considers the rise of the Medes and Persians. Deioces, who formed the Medes into a nation, built the city of Agbatana, with walls of great size and strength, which rose in circles one within the other. There were seven of these circular walls, each of which was higher than the one outside it. The outer walls were white, then black, scarlet, blue, orange, silver, and gold for the innermost sanctuary.

Here we see the beginnings of that military architecture which was to surprise the crusaders when they went to the Holy Land, and which led to our own concentric castles, like Harlech and Beaumaris in North Wales. (See Fig. 49, Vol. I., " Everyday Things in England.")

The Medes then conquered the Persians, and together they overthrew the Assyrians in 606.

The Assyrians were fine military engineers. Fig. 11 has been drawn from a sculpture in the British Museum of 884-860 B.C., which shows a walled city being taken by means of a battering-ram and siege tower of quite mediæval appearance.

We hear how the Medes and Persians were the first to give organisation to an Asiatic army, by dividing the troops into companies, with distinct bodies of spearmen, archers, and cavalry.

Also, they had no images of the gods, or temples, or altars. Herodotus explains that the Persians did not think of the gods as having the same nature as men, as the Greeks did (see p. 33).

Cyrus himself, King of Persia, had a romantic upbringing, which came about in this way. Astyages, a Mede, the son of Cyaxares, had a daughter Mandane, who married Cambyses the Persian. In due course she had a baby, and at the same time her father, Astyages, had a dream of a vine which grew so lustily that it overshadowed all Persia. This was interpreted as meaning that his grandson would reign in his stead, so it was arranged when the infant was born that it should be taken by Harpagus, a Mede, and slain—he, not liking the job, sent for a herdsman, and told him to take the child into the mountains, and there leave him to die. But the herdsman took the infant home to his wife, whose own baby had just died, and this dead baby it was which was exposed, and the live Cyrus lived to grow up and overthrow

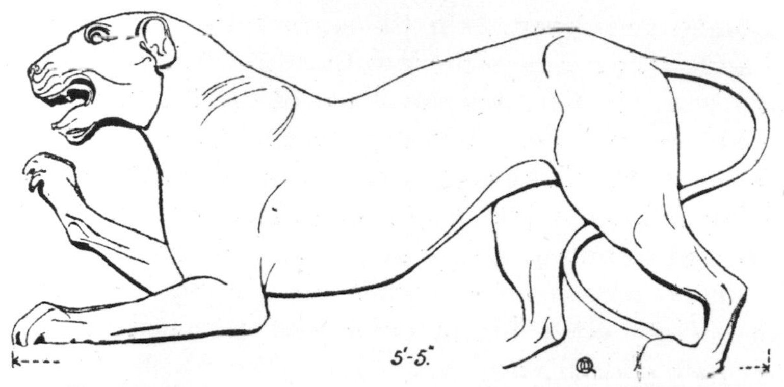

FIG. 7.—Part of a Frieze from the Acropolis at Xanthos.
(*British Museum.*)

Astyages, 553 B.C., and found the Persian Empire. The defeat of Crœsus, 547 B.C., made Cyrus master of Asia, and he then moved against the Greeks of Asia Minor. They had offered to become his lieges, but he intended their complete subjugation. They sent to Sparta for assistance, which was not given. Then they consulted the oracle at Branchidæ (p. 96).

Harpagus, a general of Cyrus, besieged the Ionian cities, using mounds. These were heaped against the walls, and so enabled the besiegers to get over them. This explains the reference in 2 Kings, chapter xix., verse 32: "Therefore thus saith the Lord concerning the king of Assyria, He shall not come into this city, nor shoot an arrow there, nor come before it with shield, nor cast a bank against it."

Herodotus tells us that Phocæa was the first city against which Harpagus directed his attack, and as well that the Phocæans of Asia Minor were the first Greeks who performed long voyages, and explored the shores of the Mediterranean as far as the city of Tartessus (near Cadiz). They used in their voyages the long penteconter (see p. 114), and not the round-built merchant-ship, and used it to good effect, for, having obtained a truce from Harpagus, they put their wives and children on board, and loaded up with their treasures, and departed for Chios; but not being allowed to settle there, some went into Corsica. In a subsequent fight with the Carthaginians many of the Phocæans were killed, and a curse descended on the slayers. On the advice of the Delphic pythoness the sin was expiated by honouring the dead Phocæans with magnificent funeral rites, and solemn games, both gymnic and equestrian.

Others followed the Phocæan example, but the inhabitants of the other Ionian cities who remained fell into servitude under Cyrus, in 545 B.C. Though the Spartans did not come to the assistance of the Ionians, they sent to Cyrus to warn him against molesting the Greeks. Cyrus' reply is interesting; he told them, "I have never yet been afraid of any men who have a set place in the middle of their city where they come together to cheat each other and forswear themselves." This was as good as telling the Spartans that they were vulgar tradesmen. The Persians apparently did not have markets. The remainder of the first book tells how Cyrus consolidated his power and took Babylon in 538. With the political history we are given many details of everyday life; for example, the Carians invented the use of crests on helmets, and handles and devices on their shields; these the Greeks copied. We hear of early town-planning when we are told that Babylon stood on a broad plain, and was an exact square.

The Babylonians had no doctors, but when a man was ill, they took him to the public square, so that the passers-by might give him the benefit of their advice, if by any chance they had had a complaint themselves which appeared to resemble his. This chapter finishes with the death of Cyrus, 529 B.C., when Cambyses succeeded to the throne.

Book II. deals with the expedition of Cambyses against Egypt, when the Ionian and Æolian Greeks were forced to accompany him as his vassals. This chapter is of the greatest interest, because it is packed with descriptions of

FIG. 8.—Part of a Frieze from Xanthos.
(*British Museum.*)

everyday life; we can give only one or two details which bear on Greece. Herodotus tells us that the land in Egypt was divided up into square plots of equal size, and let to the holders for a yearly rent. If the river carried away any portion of a man's lot, surveyors were sent to determine by measurement the exact extent of the loss, so that the rent could be adjusted. From this practice, geometry first came to be known in Egypt, whence it passed into Greece. The sundial, however, and the gnomon, with the division of the day into twelve parts, came to the Greeks from Babylon. Another interesting detail is, that Herodotus, while he was travelling in Egypt, was told by the priests another version of the Trojan War. After the rape of Helen, an army of Greeks sailed to Troy, and demanded the restoration of Helen and the treasures taken with her. The Trojans replied that they could not do this, as both had been taken to Egypt. The Greeks did not believe them, and laid siege to the town, but when they took it, could not find Helen. Menelaus, Helen's husband, was then sent to Egypt, where he found his wife at the Court of Proteus. Herodotus adds that he thinks this was what really did happen, and not the version Homer told.

Herodotus gives us an example of Persian justice. Cambyses, hearing that one of his judges had been bribed, killed and flayed him, and cutting his skin into strips, used it for the seat of the justice throne. The judge's son was appointed in his stead, and told to remember always how his seat was cushioned.

Book III. deals with the conquest of Egypt by Cambyses (525 B.C.), the son of Cyrus, and of his madness and death, and how he was succeeded by Darius.

Book IV. opens with the words, " After the taking of Babylon, an expedition was led by Darius into Scythia," but we are not given any details of this for some time. Herodotus evidently thought that his readers, who would know the positions of Persia and Egypt, might yet be doubtful about Scythia, so the chapter is very interesting, because it gives an idea of early geography. Herodotus thought of Greece as the centre of the world. India was the limit of the inhabited world on the east—Arabia and Libya (Africa) towards the south. Of the north and west Herodotus did not seem to know anything, and could never obtain any assurance from an eye-witness that there was sea " on the farther side of Europe." He had heard of the Cassiterides, or Tin Islands (it is thought that these may have been the British Isles), and knew that tin and amber came to the Mediterranean, apparently from the ends of the earth.

Herodotus knew that Africa was surrounded by the sea, except for the neck where the Suez Canal is, and even this latter had been attempted before his time. Seti I., in the fourteenth century B.C., cut a canal and joined the Nile and the Red Sea. This was enlarged by Necho, 612 B.C., and after this he sent ships down the Red Sea to sail around Africa. The crew sailed south all along the east coast and, doubling the Cape, came up by the west coast. When they ran out of food they landed and sowed corn, and, waiting for it to grow and ripen, sailed on again after their harvest. In the third year they came to the Pillars of Hercules (the Straits of Gibraltar), and so to their own Mediterranean Sea.

Herodotus by this time had sketched in the outlines of his picture. In the foreground are the tiny Greek city states of Ionia, surrounded by powerful neighbours like Assyria, Persia, and Egypt. All of them were in a measure civilised, and dwelt within a small compass. We need reminder of how small a world the Greek world was, and how on the outskirts were barbarians. So Herodotus next traces the journey of Darius by way of the Bosphorus, up the west coast of the Black Sea, to the Scythian lands where people lived who were prepared to swoop down, like the later Huns, and blot out civilisation. He tells us that they had neither cities nor forts, but were nomads living in their travelling wagons. They could all shoot from horseback, and lived, not by husbandry, but on their cattle.

The Scythian drank the blood of the first man he killed in battle, and cut off all the heads of the remainder and carried them to his king, who was entitled to share the booty, unless he failed to produce at least one head himself. The head was scalped by making a cut round it above the ears, and shaking out the skull. The scalp was used as a napkin, and was hung from the bridle-rein. If the Scythian had good hunting, the scalps were sewn together to make cloaks. Another amiable habit was to flay the right arms of their dead enemies, and tan the skin, with the nails hanging to it, and use it as a covering for their quivers. It is interesting to know that the skin of a man is thick and glossy, and whiter than the other hides. They treated the skulls of those whom they most detested as follows: having sawn off the portion below the eyebrows, the inside was cleaned out, and the outside covered with leather and used as a drinking-cup. If they wanted to make a good job of it, the inside was lined with gold.

When they took an oath, the parties to it took a large earthen bowl and filled it with wine, and then, wounding themselves, they allowed some of their blood to drop into the wine; then a scimitar, some arrows, a battle-axe, and a javelin were plunged in it: meanwhile prayers were said; then the two drank each a draught of the mixture.

In the funerals of their kings the body was laid in the grave, stretched upon a mattress; spears were fixed in the ground on either side of the corpse, and supported beams stretched across above to form a roof, which was covered with thatch. Around the body of the king they buried one of his concubines, first killed by strangulation, and also his cup-bearer, cook, groom, lackey, messenger, some of his horses, firstlings of all his other possessions, and some golden cups; and then a great mound was raised above the grave.

The Scythian women had an amusing way of cleansing themselves which sounds worth a trial. Cypress, cedar, and frankincense wood was pounded into a paste, with a little water, to a thick consistency. This substance they plastered over their whole bodies. And when on the following day they took off the plaster, their skin was clean and glossy, and a sweet odour had been imparted to them.

The Sauromatæ, neighbours of the Scythians, allowed none of the girls to marry until she had first killed a man in battle.

The Scythians, not having any cities, moved about their country in wagons, and could not be brought to battle by the Persians, so the campaign was indecisive, 514 B.C.

FIG. 9.—Part of a Frieze from Xanthos.
(British Museum.)

There followed the Persian expeditions to Libya, which again is outside our subject, except that Herodotus gives interesting details of the Greek settlements at Cyrene, on the north coast of Africa. We must bear in mind that emigrants from the homeland went not only to Ionia but to nearly all the Mediterranean coast lands.

The Persians besieged Barca, another Greek city, for nine months, and drove several mines from their own lines to the walls. Their mines were discovered by a brass worker, inside the city, who went round with a brazen shield and laid it on the ground. Where the ground was undermined the brass of the shield rang, but in the other places the shield, when he laid it down, was quite dumb. The Barceans counter-mined, and slew the Persian diggers.

Herodotus tells one tale which shows how primitive trade was carried on by the Carthaginians, relating that they used to visit a people in Libya, beyond the Pillars of Hercules (that would be on the west coast of Africa), where, when they arrived, they unloaded their wares, and set them out in an orderly fashion on the beach, and then returned aboard their ships and raised a great smoke. When the natives saw the smoke, they came down to the shore, and looking over the goods, put down as much gold as they thought they were worth, and then withdrew to a distance. The Carthaginians then came ashore, and if they thought the gold enough, took it and sailed away; if not, they retired aboard ship once more and waited for more gold, and so on, until both sides were content. The natives never ran away with the goods, nor did the Carthaginians take them back and run off with the gold.

The *FIFTH BOOK* gives the early history of Sparta, and details of the Persian expedition to Pæonia in Thrace. Here in the country to the north-east of the mainland of Greece the Persians found lake dwellers. These people lived like the dwellers in the Swiss lake villages, of which we wrote in Volume II. of the "Everyday Life" Series, and which had many points of resemblance with our own Glastonbury lake village. Herodotus gives details of these Thracian lake dwellings—of how the piles were driven into the bed of the lake to support the platforms on which the huts were built, and approached by a single narrow bridge; how trap-doors gave access to the lake underneath, and the fish were so plentiful that all you had to do was to lower a basket into which the fish came and very conveniently packed themselves, all ready to be drawn up. Not only the people, but the horses, ate the fish. The babies were tied up with a string by the foot.

During this campaign the Persians consolidated their powers in the Ægean. They took the islands of Lemnos and Imbros, and Herodotus notes that up till this time not one of the Cyclades (the islands in the Ægean Sea) was subject to King Darius. It was told to him that Naxos was fertile, and containing much treasure and many slaves. Slaves, unfortunately, were an essential part of Greek civilisation. They supplied the man power which was necessary before the days of "horse-power." So a Persian expedition was sent to annex Naxos. This was a failure because of the brutal treatment by the Persians of a captain of an auxiliary ship, whose friends, in consequence, warned the people of Naxos. Forewarned was forearmed, so that they were able to beat off the Persians and remain masters of the sea.

Before this a Persian general had advised the king, after he had conquered all the Cyclades, to send a hundred ships to annex Eubœa, the large island which nearly touches the east coast of the mainland of Greece, and had his advice been followed, the history of Western Europe would have followed a different course. The Cyclades are stepping-stones across the Ægean, and Eubœa a jumping-off place from where the subjugation of Greece itself could have been accomplished. Fortunately for us the advice was not followed.

The failure of the expedition to Naxos led to a revolt of the Ionian cities against the Persians. The conspirators chose a clever way to communicate with one another. The head of a slave was shaved and the message tattooed on the bare skull. The hair was allowed to grow, and the slave was sent with a message that his head was to be shaved and then read.

The Spartans were asked to render assistance, "inasmuch as the pre-eminence over all Greece appertains to you," and here it was that Aristagoras, pleading with Cleomenes on behalf of the Ionians, attempted to bribe the Spartan, and, offering at first ten talents, increased it step by step to fifty, when Gorgo, the daughter of Cleomenes, interrupted and said, "Father, get up and go, or the stranger will certainly corrupt you." And so Aristagoras was sent away, and no help given him. He then sailed to Athens, because "he knew that, after Sparta, Athens was the most powerful of the Grecian states." The Athenians voted that twenty ships should be sent to the assistance of the Ionians. As Herodotus points out, this was the beginning of the trouble which culminated at Salamis. The Ionian revolt failed, and Darius asked who the Athenians were, and on being told, took his bow and shot an arrow into the sky, and called on his god that he might be revenged on the Athenians. He also commanded a servant to say to him three times each day, when at dinner, "Master, remember the Athenians."

There are many interesting details in the *FIFTH BOOK.* We are told that it was the Phœnicians who introduced writing into Greece.

There is an interesting note on clothes. The Athenians sent an expedition to Ægina, which met with disaster, and only one survivor came back to Athens. The wives of all those who had been killed crowded round the man, and struck him with the brooches by which their dresses were fastened, asking him, "Where is my husband?" And the man died. The Athenians thought the deed so horrible that they changed the dress of their women from the Dorian type (Fig. 47), which required brooches, to the Ionian linen tunic, which was sewn, and so did not require brooches (see Fig. 48).

Book VI. deals with the conditions after the revolt of the Ionians. Herodotus gives one very interesting detail. Phrynichus, a poet, produced a drama in Athens on the Capture of Miletus (one of the Ionian cities captured

FIG. 10.—From the Walls of a Tomb at Xanthos, *c.* 470 B.C.
(*British Museum.*)

by the Persians). This so affected the Athenian audience that all the people burst into tears, and the unfortunate poet was fined 1,000 drachms for being too tragic an artist. The Persians, who at first treated the Ionians cruelly, after some time did them no more hurt, but summoning deputies from the cities, compelled them to enter into treaties not to quarrel with one another. Others sailed away—some to Zancle, the modern Messina. Like our own William the Conqueror, Darius compiled a Doomsday survey, measuring up their country in parasangs (30 furlongs).

Having finished with the Ionians, Darius had time to deal with the Athenians, and we have heard the precautions that he took that he should not forget. We may be quite sure that every time Darius sat down to dinner his servant said to him three times, " Master, remember the Athenians " —it was not advisable to forget the instructions of a Persian king. So an expedition was sent against them, 493 B.C., under Mardonius, who had married the king's daughter. The fleet skirted the land while the army marched to the Hellespont, crossing which, they proceeded through Thrace and Macedonia. A storm drove many of the ships against Mount Athos, and this expedition failed (see Fig. 2).

Darius does not appear to have been perturbed. It

must have been inconceivable to him that these Athenians, of whom he knew so little, could oppose him, so he made preparations for another expedition, and sent heralds to Greece to demand submission, but Themistocles had foreseen the trouble ahead and was already fortifying the Peiræus.

The second Persian expedition, under Datis, 490 B.C., remembering how their ships had been wrecked on Mount Athos the year before, embarked the troops and horses on the fleet, and sailed across to Greece by Samos and the islands of the Cyclades, their destination being Eretria, on the Attica side of Eubœa, the large island off the east coast of Greece—a much more dangerous threat. Ionians and Æolians were forced to accompany the Persians. The Athenians came to the rescue of the Eretrians, but, hearing that some were for flight, and others for betraying their country to the Persians, withdrew to Oropus. The Persians defeated the Eretrians, and then sailed to Marathon, on the mainland of Greece, not many miles from Athens itself. The Athenians, under Miltiades, sent the runner Pheidippides to Sparta to ask for help, and he took only two days to run 135 to 140 miles; but the Spartans had to wait until the full of the moon before they could help. Meanwhile the Athenians drew themselves up in order of battle in the sacred close of Heracles, with the Platæans who came to their aid on their left wing. Herodotus says that the Greeks charged the Persians at a run, and that this was the first time that the Greeks employed the charge. The centre of the Greek line was broken, but the two wings outflanked and outfought the Persians, and drove them back to their ships, and captured seven of these. The Greeks had won the first round against their great adversary.

In the *SIXTH BOOK* we are told of the honours accorded to the Spartan kings at death; of how, when the women heard the news which was carried by horsemen, they ran hither and thither, drumming on kettles, and when these were heard, in every house two free persons, a man and a woman, had to put on mourning, and the three types of people had to attend the funeral. There were the Spartans, descended from the Dorians and Heracles himself; the country people, descended probably from the dispossessed Achæans who had submitted to the Spartans; and the Helots, who were the slaves. They spoke of the Dorian Invasion (of which we wrote on p. 1) as the "Return of the Heracleidæ."

There is another note on the use of wine. The Spartans thought the madness of Cleomenes was caused by his having learned to drink his wine without water from Scythians who came to Sparta. The Greeks always diluted their wine with water.

There is another note explaining the use of tallies. A certain Milesian came to Sparta, and brought half his money with him, because Ionia was insecure, while Sparta stood firm. He gave the money into the hands of Glaucus, with tallies, saying that he must not give the money to anyone unless they brought the fellows of the tallies. These tallies were short sticks which were notched and then split, the Milesian keeping one half and Glaucus the other, and he would know if the Milesian had really sent his half, because the notches on the two when put together would tally.

As to marriage, Callias was held to be remarkable, because he had three daughters, and when they came to be of marriageable age, he gave each of them a dowry, and allowed them to choose their own husbands. The usual practice seems to have been followed by Clisthenes, another father, who had a daughter called Agarista, whom he wished to marry to the best husband that he could find in the whole of Greece. At the Olympic Games, therefore, having gained the prize in the chariot race, he caused public proclamation to be made that any Greek who deemed himself worthy to become the son-in-law of Clisthenes, should come within sixty days to Sicyon; for within a year's time Clisthenes would decide on the man to whom he should contract his daughter. Suitors began to flock in, and Clisthenes had a foot-course and a wrestling-ground made ready, to try their powers. He kept them on tenter-hooks for a whole year, but the favourite appears to have been an Athenian, Hippoclides, the son of Tisander.

The day at length arrived when Clisthenes had to declare his choice. First of all he sacrificed a hundred oxen, and held a banquet for all the suitors and the people of Sicyon. After the feast the suitors showed how well they could play and speak on a given subject, and then, as the drinking advanced, Hippoclides called for the flute-player, and began to dance. Clisthenes, so Herodotus tells us, began to feel very unhappy. Then Hippoclides, not content, told an attendant to bring in a table, and mounting upon it, danced first of all some Laconian figures, then some Attic ones, and then, throwing away discretion, he stood on his head upon the table and began to toss his legs about. This was more than Clisthenes could stand, and he cried out, " Son of Tisander, thou hast danced thy wife away! " " What does Hippoclides care? " was the other's answer, and so the Greek proverb arose.

The *SEVENTH BOOK* opens with a note that when the news of the Battle of Marathon reached King Darius, his anger against the Athenians waxed still fiercer, and he became more than ever eager to lead an army against Greece. He died, however, 485 B.C., before he was able to do so, and the task was left to his son Xerxes. First a revolt in Egypt had to be subdued, 484 B.C., and Xerxes then reconsidered the question of the attack on Greece, the land of " the Ionians who live in Europe." His uncle tried to persuade him against the expedition. Xerxes

FIG. 11.—The Siege of a Walled City in Assyria.
(Reconstruction from Sculptures in Assyrian Gallery, British Museum.)

first decided to go, then altered his mind, and finally was sent to meet his fate by a dream. He spent four full years collecting his host from all the nations in Asia. Detachments from the tributary nations were sent to cut a canal "beneath the lash of taskmasters," through the Isthmus of Acte, off the Macedonian coast, 12 furlongs long, so as to save the rough passage through the stormy waters rounding Mount Athos, where the fleet had been wrecked in the expedition under Mardonius. Herodotus tells us that only the Phœnicians understood what is meant by the " angle of repose " of material. They cut their part with sloping sides, so that the earth did not tumble in on them. A bridge of boats was built across the Hellespont, but a great storm broke the whole work to pieces. " When Xerxes heard of this he gave orders that the Hellespont should receive three hundred lashes, and that a pair of fetters be cast into it," and the bridge was repaired.

It was at Abydos, on the Hellespont, that Xerxes reviewed his troops. The whole Hellespont was covered with the vessels of his fleet, and all the shore and every plain about Abydos was full of troops. Xerxes, after reviewing his army, wept, saying to Artabanus, " There came upon me a sudden pity, when I thought of the shortness of man's life, and considered that of all this host, so numerous as it is, not one will be alive when a hundred years are gone by."

After Xerxes had crossed the bridge of boats he stood to contemplate his army as they crossed " under the lash." The crossing took seven days and seven nights.

There is an interesting note on the difficulty which these early people found in counting. Xerxes wanted to count his army, and this is the way he went to work. Ten thousand men were made to stand as close together as possible, and then a circle was drawn round them. On the circle a fence was built about the height of a man's middle. Then the enclosure was filled continually with fresh troops, till the whole army had been counted.

When the Persians reached the River Strymon in Macedonia, they sacrificed white horses to make the stream favourable to their crossing, and then arrived at a place called The Nine Ways (after Amphipolis)—here, learning

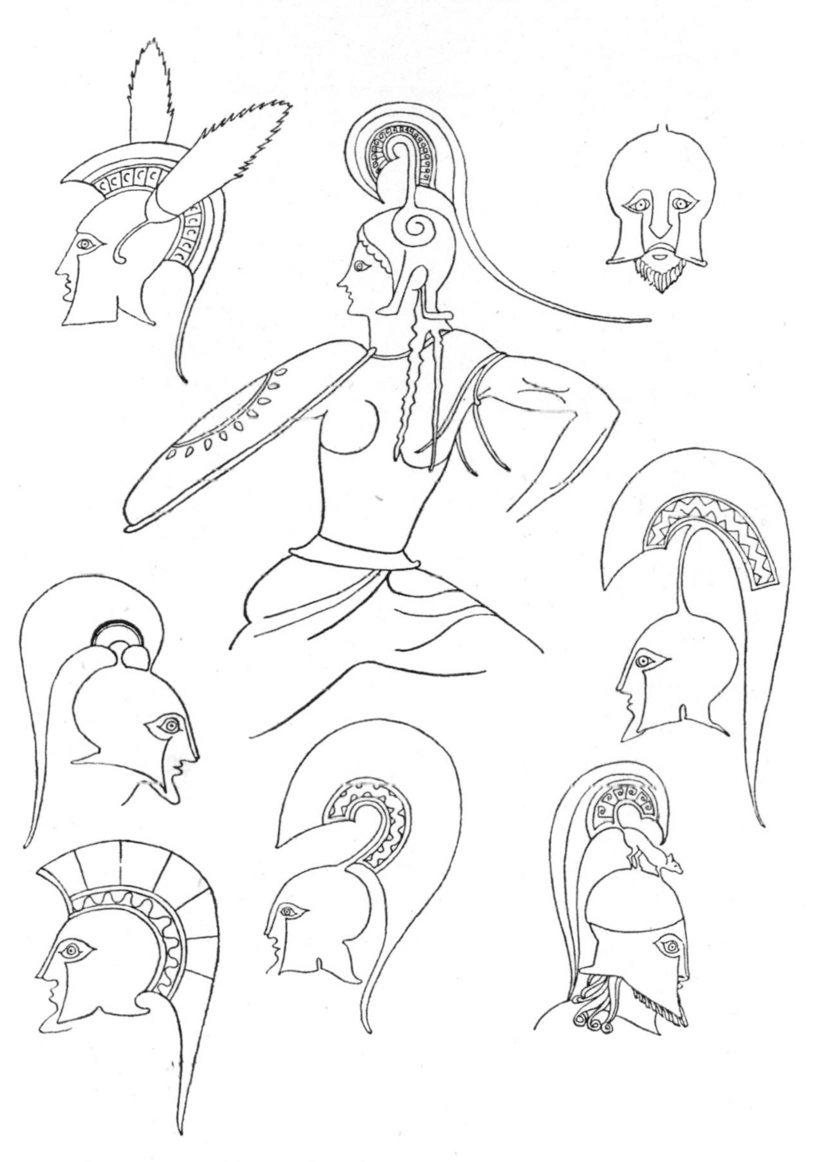

FIG. 12.—Helmets and Crests from Black-Figure Vases, Sixth Century B.C.
(*British Museum.*)

the name of the place, they took nine of the youths of the land, and as many of their maidens, and buried them alive on the spot, as a sacrifice to the god dwelling underneath the earth.

The Persian navy, skirting the shore, sailed through the channel which had been cut by Mount Athos, and had brushes with scouting ships sent out from Athens, and the Persians succeeded in taking two of these. The news of the disaster was sent from the island of Sciathus to Artemisium (about thirteen miles) by fire signals.

The ships were not very large, because Herodotus tells us how some of the Persians, on one occasion, saved both themselves and their vessels by dragging them up on the beach. A great storm destroyed part of Xerxes' fleet off Cape Sepias, and it took refuge in the Bay of Pagasæ.

On the recommendation of the men of Thessaly, the Greeks sent a force to guard the Pass of Olympus, where they occupied the defile of Tempe, but this force was recalled, so that the Thessalians were compelled to join Xerxes.

He sent heralds to many of the other Greek cities, demanding that they should send him earth and water as a sign of their submission. No heralds were sent to Athens or Sparta, and the Greek force was now drawn up at the Pass of Thermopylæ, their fleet being at Artemisium, on the north coast of Eubœa.

The *SEVENTH BOOK* closes with a description of the fight at Thermopylæ (the Hot Gates) and the end of the Spartans, who were seen by a spy of Xerxes combing their hair before the battle. The Persians, driven on by whips, were unable to take the Pass by frontal attack, but did so in the end, because they were shown a path over the mountains by Ephialtes. The main body of the Greeks retreated, and the Spartans remained to hold the Persians in check. Of their last fight, under Leonidas, and how they defended themselves with swords, and then, when these were broken, with hands and teeth, until the last of them, surrounded on all sides, were overwhelmed and buried under showers of missiles, we cannot give the details, but this is one of the great heroic tales of history.

Things had now reached a desperate pass for the Greeks, and all the comfort they had was a message from the Delphic oracle that—

> " Safe shall the wooden wall continue for thee and thy children.
> Wait not the tramp of the horse, nor the footmen mightily moving
> Over the land, but turn your back to the foe, and retire ye."

Some of the Greeks thought this meant they were to desert Athens and take to their ships. This was the view of Themistocles and this is what they did, the Greek navy by this time having retreated from Artemisium to Salamis.

After Thermopylæ, the main body of the Persians came down through Bœotia to Athens, which they burned. The Persian fleet by this time had come down south through the Euripus, the narrow strait between Eubœa and the mainland, to Phalerum, near Athens.

Now the stage was set for the last act of the great drama, and it seemed as if nothing could save the Greeks from the might of Persia. Yet Herodotus clearly thinks that the gods were on the side of the Greeks, because he tells us how, before Salamis, a cloud of dust such as might be raised by a crowd of 30,000 men was seen coming from Eleusis. From the cloud came the sound of voices, chanting the mystic hymn to Bacchus, which was sung at the festival to Demeter and Persephone at Eleusis, and the cloud sailed in the direction of Salamis, and rested over the Greek fleet. So, comforted by their gods, the Greeks braced themselves, and in the *EIGHTH BOOK* Herodotus reaches the peak of his history and tells how the Persians were defeated at the Battle of Salamis, 480 B.C. The Persians were not a seafaring nation, and their fleet, manned by Phœnicians, Cyprians, Ionians, and Egyptians, was no match for that of the Greeks in its own home waters. Still, the might of Persia had been so great that, when the sea fight was over, the Greeks, first setting all the wrecked and disabled ships together, prepared for another engagement, thinking that Xerxes would renew the fight with the vessels which still remained to him. But the king had no more heart left in him, and feared that the Greeks might sail straight to the Hellespont and break down the bridges there, in which case he would be blocked up in Europe, and run great risk of perishing. He therefore made up his mind to fly. At the precise moment that Xerxes came to this decision, the whole course of Western civilisation was altered, and it was left to the Greeks to steer the way. So we can take leave of the Persian king. Herodotus gives one amusing detail of him: A great banquet was given on his birthday, and gifts distributed, "and this is the only day in all the year on which the King soaps his head."

The *NINTH BOOK* deals with the fate of the remainder of the Persian army, left behind by Xerxes under the command of Mardonius, and how they were defeated at Platæa, 479 B.C. The folly of the whole enterprise was well shown by Pausanias, the Spartan commander, who captured the war tent of Xerxes, which had been left behind for the use of Mardonius. This was adorned with gold and silver; its hangings were of divers colours. Pausanias ordered the Persian cooks to make ready for him a feast in such fashion as was their wont for Mardonius. And this they did. The couches were of gold and silver, with rich coverings. The tables of gold and silver were laid with a feast which suited such magnificence. Then Pausanias ordered his own followers to prepare a Spartan supper. Then both suppers were served, and it was apparent how vast a difference lay between the two, and Pausanias laughed, and sent for the Greek generals, and pointed to the two boards, and said: "I sent for you, O Greeks, to show you the folly of this Median captain, who, when he enjoyed such fare as this, must needs come here to rob us of our penury."

FIG. 13.
Device on a Shield.

Here our outline from Herodotus must end. We leave him with the Greeks triumphant. There must have been a period after Salamis when they rested to lick their wounds and get the ache of battle out of their bones. Perhaps they wondered how it had all happened. Their thoughts may have gone back to the time when their forefathers had been turned out of Greece by the Dorians. They may have remembered their wanderings and struggles in Ionia and the other Greek colonies, and the tales of the heroes, and the traditions of Mycenæan art which they took with them. They may have realised, as Herodotus did, that the Arts and Sciences were kept alive in these colonies, and in due course, when the colonists sent heralds to consult the oracles in Delphi, or athletes to compete in the Games at Olympia, these returning Greeks carried back with them something indefinable, which quickened the Greek genius again. Homer sustained them, and as they heard the "Iliad," they remembered that they were descended from heroes, and the adventures of Odysseus sent them out in search of adventure themselves. They were quarrelsome, and not always helpful to one another—sometimes they were treacherous—they were undisciplined, and yet overthrew the disciplined host of Persia, and in a few short years after Salamis were able to raise a structure of art and science which was so wonderful and so much in the highest class that we call it to-day "Classical." How this was done must always be one of the wonders of history. Perhaps it was because, for the first time, men were allowed to think and express their innermost thoughts in speech or writing—so the thoughts and ideas flowered, and formed Classical Greece. But we shall never enjoy the beauty of the flowering unless we are prepared to take some little trouble in finding out how the plant itself grew, and the qualities of the soil which nourished its roots.

CHAPTER II.—THE TEMPLE AND THE HOUSE

We will now examine the architectural accomplishments of the Greeks in the Archaic period, which came to an end with the Battle of Salamis in 480 B.C.

The first thing to be noted is that they had two patterns of building, one we call Doric and the other Ionic, and these correspond with the two great divisions of the Greek race. The Spartans were the typical Dorians, and the Achæans, who fled to Asia Minor, were the Ionians.

We will deal with the Doric type of architecture now, and take the temple first, because it was in housing their gods that the Greeks expended their greatest energies.

To understand the temple, we must realise that the religion of the Greeks was quite different to that of the Christians. Herodotus noted (p. 10) how the Persians did not think of the gods as having the same nature as men, as the Greeks did. The Christian believes that "God said, Let us make man in our image, after our likeness" (Genesis i).

This is the essential thing about Greek religion, that instead of man being made in the image of God, the gods were like men, only being stronger, cleverer, and braver, they were better able to look after themselves, and settle all the difficult problems which arise when man himself seeks to interpret the Universe.

So when the lightning flashed, and the thunder rumbled and echoed in the mountains, the Greek called on Father Zeus, who lived on cloud-capped Olympus. Or, if he was at sea in one of his fragile boats, and the waves arose, then Poseidon would help him. If his lady-love would not smile, Aphrodite would know how to soften her heart. Hera, the wife of Zeus, was capricious and feminine. Hades was the god of the dead. Hestia guarded the hearth, and

Demeter was the corn spirit. They were the brothers and sisters of Zeus. Then he had children, just as the Greeks had. Athene was the goddess of the Arts; Apollo the god of light; Hermes the messenger; Dionysus the god of the vine; Aphrodite of love; Hephæstos of fire; and Ares of war.

All these relationships were regularised by Hesiod between 750 and 700 B.C., and we wrote of this in Vol. I. So the Greek had gods on whom he could rely for help on any occasion, and they were fellow Greeks, and, as such, understood the nature of a bargain. All the gods demanded was that they should be propitiated by sacrifice. This done, the Greek was safe. He was not oppressed by any feeling of sin, or that he need save his soul. Like an eagle, he could soar in his quest of beauty. The modern man, alas, too often and quite unnecessarily, has thought of himself as a worm, and, oppressed by sin, has been confined in a two-dimensional world.

The first thing to remember, then, is that the temple was the house of the god they worshipped, and, as such, it had to be finer than the house of man. It was not a church, as we understand it, used for a congregation of people worshipping inside the building.

We can now consider the various type of temples, and here we cannot do better than turn to Vitruvius, a Roman, and the first of the writing architects, who published his book on architecture in the time of Augustus, 27 B.C. to 14 A.D. It is obvious that he had made a study of Greek architecture, and as one of the Roman architects he would have to do so, because their inspiration came from Greece. So far as Western Europe is concerned, only Greek and Gothic architecture have been primary styles, all the others have been derived from these. Vitruvius probably invented the technical terms, and he seems to have been fairly good at it. We have drawn Fig. 14, which will show that

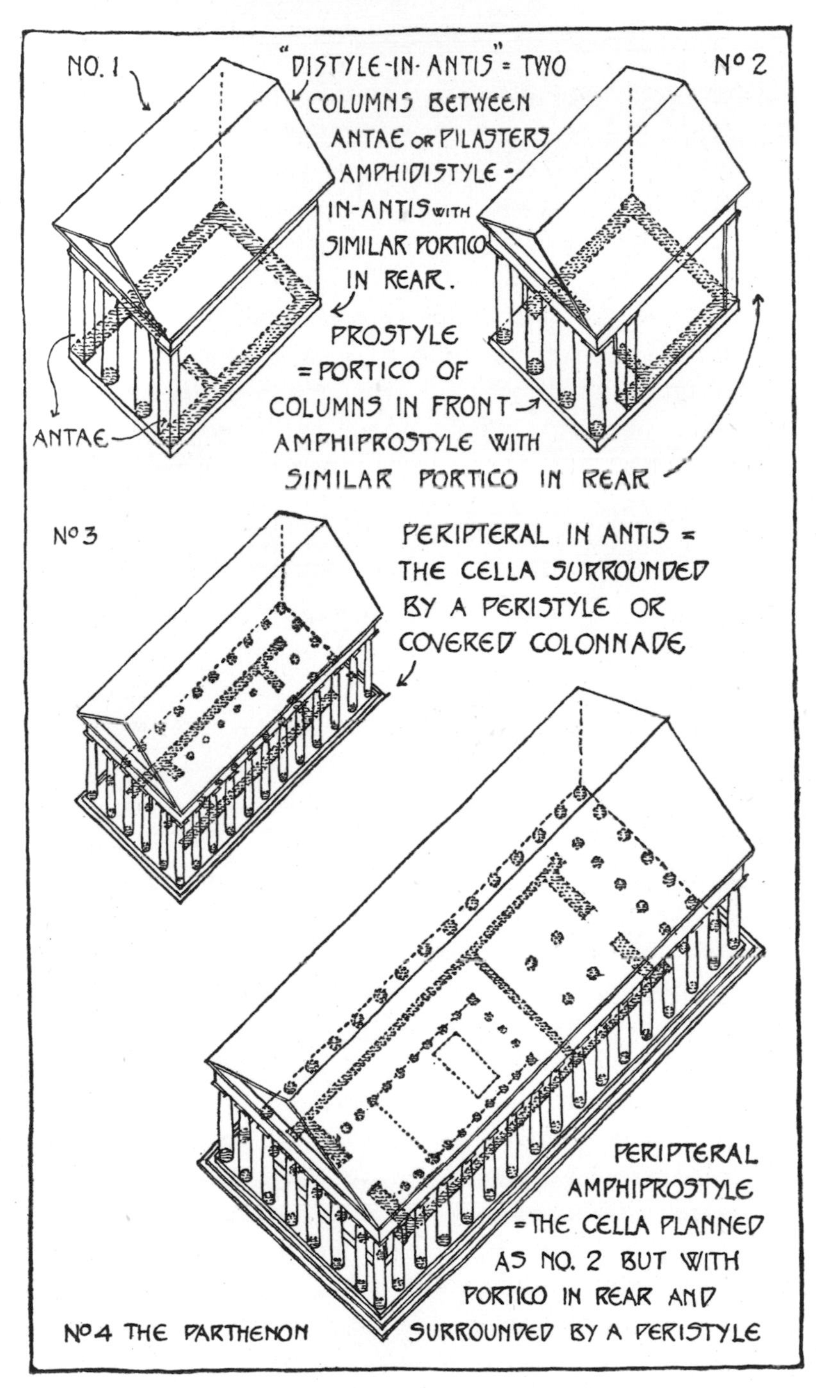

FIG. 14.—Types of Temples.

"Peripteral Amphiprostyle" is not really so alarming as it sounds at first. The simplest type of temple had the cella, which contained the image of the god, with a porch before it, as No. 1, Fig. 14. Nos. 2 and 3 show how this was developed. In the fully developed temple, as the Parthenon, No. 4, Fig. 14, there was the porch (pronaos) in front of the cella, which faced east, and a chamber at the back, which was used as a treasury where offerings to the god could be put, and this had another porch (opisthodomus), the whole group being surrounded by a colonnaded walk.

If reference is made to Fig. 57, Vol. I., "Homeric Greece," of the plan of the Men's Hall at Tiryns, built by the Achæans who invaded Greece about 1450 B.C., and again to Fig. 1, of the Argos Hut of the eighth century B.C., it will be seen that the Greek temple of the Archaic period was clearly a descendant of the early homes of men. This continued in Greek and Roman classical times; the gods continued to live in halls, as did the Achæan chieftain, long after their descendants had altered the patterns of their own houses. In the same way, because the first figures of the gods were cut in wood, they continued to be made in this way; even in the Parthenon, the great figure of Athene was made of wood, though it was sheathed with gold and ivory.

To go back to the temple plan. We see the ruins of one to-day set in solitude; a few columns support a broken architrave against the blue sky, and we walk amongst the scattered stones and find it difficult to reconstruct it as a centre of life. Originally a wall surrounded the sacred enclosure. There was a great altar outside the east porch where sacrifice could be offered, and the god worshipped by the people, standing with raised arms and the palms of their hands uppermost. If they prayed to the gods of the underworld, the hands were reversed. If the temple was in a great shrine, sacred to all the Greeks, as at Delphi, then the various other cities would have their own treasuries in the enclosure, where the vestments they used at festivals could be stored, and the precincts would be beautified by statues and all kinds of works of art sent as offerings to the gods. We shall attempt to describe Delphi in Vol. III.; meanwhile we are concerned with the development of Doric architecture.

First, we must try to understand the principles which guided the Doric architects, and we can explain what we mean by principles by the following tale. During 1929, an article appeared in a newspaper about a big hotel to be built in London, which was being designed by an engineer. The engineer intended to show the architects how to build; there were to be no frills. The hotel was to be constructed on lines as efficient and scientific as those which go to produce an aeroplane, or a dynamo, or the Parthenon. He was a foolish engineer to drag in the Parthenon, because the great Doric temple, which was built in Athens, on the Acropolis, and which has been regarded through all the years since as one of the most wonderful and beautiful buildings of the world, was not constructed on lines of efficiency. It was really timber construction carried out in marble; from the engineer's own point of view, rather a dishonest building—a wanton beauty.

To go back to the Doric architects: they were sticklers for tradition. It is obvious that the actual ground on which the temple stood was sacred. Greek architects were frequently hampered in this way. Their buildings often had to be placed in a certain spot, or were cut short because they might encroach on another sacred area.

Then the actual form of the temple became sanctified by use. As we have pointed out, the Megaron at Tiryns, and the Argos Hut, are obviously in the same building tradition, and this form became established as the temple type. One of the earliest Doric temples of which ruins remain was that dedicated to Hera, at Olympia; this dates from about 700 B.C., and there were two earlier temples on the same site. The cella walls had stone bases of great thickness, faced on the outside with vertical slabs (orthostates) as a dado. On this stone base the upper walls were built of sun-dried mud bricks. It was these bricks which preserved the Hermes of Praxiteles, which is now in the museum at Olympia; this statue was found at the foot of its pedestal, buried in clay formed out of the brick walls which had fallen in and covered it. The columns of this early temple at Olympia were formed of wood, as they were at Tiryns.

Here we must introduce another great name in Greek history, Pausanias, a native of Lydia, who travelled extensively, and wrote his "Descriptions of Greece," between about 150-175 A.D. He writes that in his time one of the pillars of the back chamber of the temple of Hera at Olympia was of oak. From this it is conjectured that the entablature, and the columns which supported it, were originally of wood, the latter being replaced with stone as they decayed. Fig. 15 has been drawn to show this timber construction of the early Doric temples, and Fig. 16, of the Temple of Theseus in Athens, shows how the timber forms survived even when stone and marble were used for building. Let us take Fig. 15 first, and we will start with the timber shaft cut from a sturdy oak. It would have been a reasonable thing for a carpenter to place a circular pad on the top of the shaft, with a good square block of wood over it. These became the Echinus and Abacus (see Fig. 16). The purpose of the vertical columns was to support beams, bridged across horizontally from column to column; these became the architraves. Having obtained a beam all round the building, then others were placed across the building with their ends resting on the architrave. These tied the whole building together and provided it with a ceiling. The ends of the beams were chamfered off to make them look nice, and so one arrived at the triglyphs, as Fig. 16. One of these cross-beams always came over the top of the column under, and one between the columns, so that spaces were left between the beams on the top of the architrave.

These were filled in with brick at the back, and at first terra-cotta panels were placed in front of the bricks, later beautifully carved marble panels were inserted, as at the Parthenon, and became the metopes. On the top of all this another beam was placed, to give good fixing for the ends of the overhanging rafters. Later these became part of the marble cornice, and were called mutules, as Fig. 16, but the little wooden pegs used when they were of wood continued to be shown in the new material, and the mutules still sloped as they had when they were the feet of rafters. It is the architrave, frieze, and cornice which together are called the entablature.

Sometimes the wooden mouldings of these early temples were sheathed with gaily decorated terra-cotta plaques.

At the ends of the building the sloping roofs were finished with flat gables, called pediments. Along the tops of these a gutter, or sima, ran, which finished at the feet with a lion's head. The roof was covered with thatch in the earliest times, and then, later, with terra-cotta and marble tiles resting on the rafters; these were flat, with turned-up edges at the sides which were placed together, and covered with a small tile which had a pretty little termination at the eaves, called an antefix. In the later Ionic temples the sima was continued along the sides of the building, as a gutter, with lions' heads as waterspouts. Acroteria were the ornaments placed on the apex and at the feet of the pediments. The temples had ceilings inside,

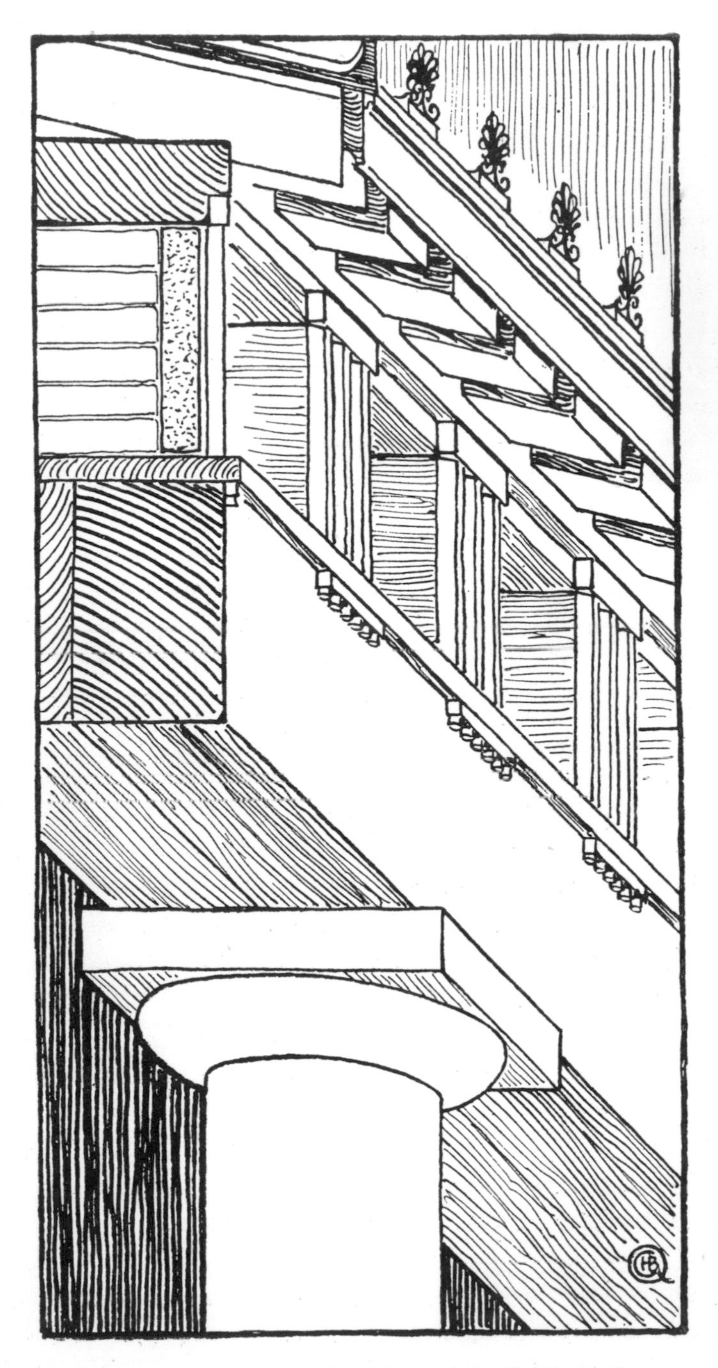

Fig. 15.—The Timber Origin of the Doric Style.

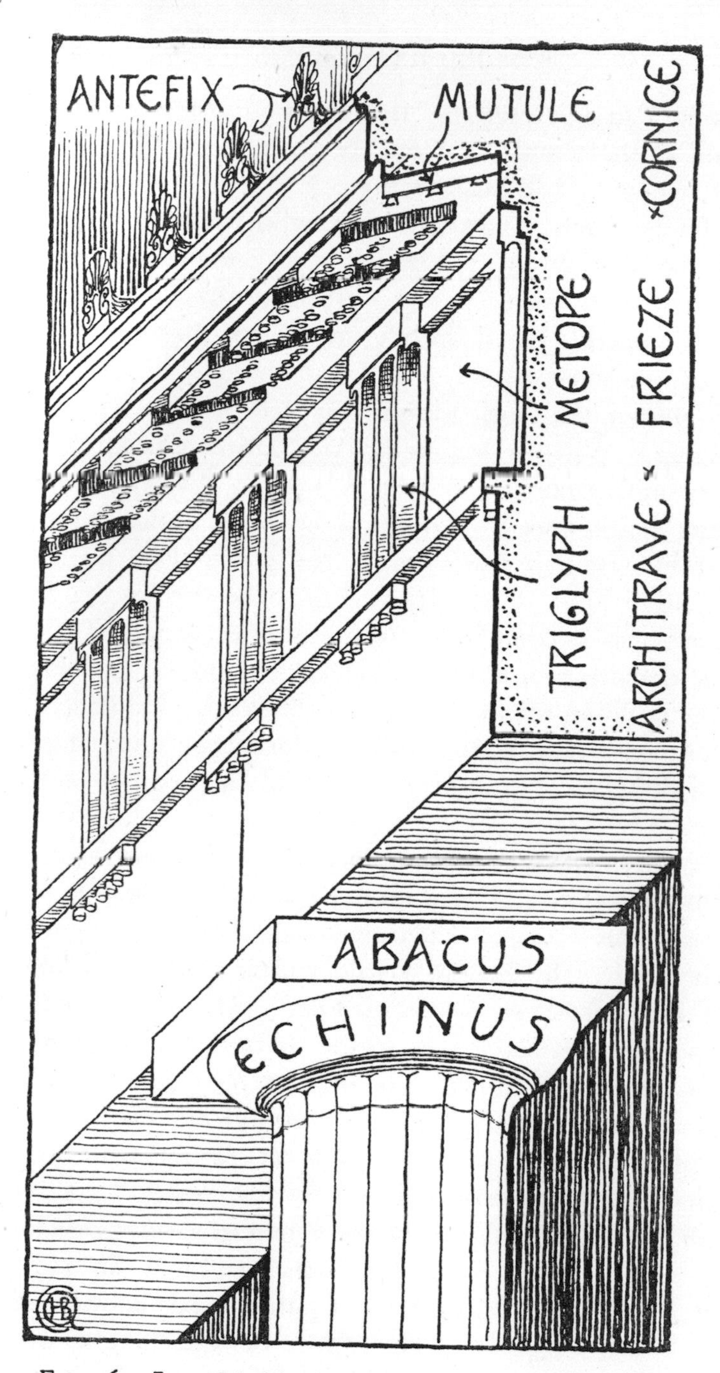

Fig. 16.—Later Marble Construction of the Doric Style.

because Pausanias tells us that the body of a soldier was found at the temple of Hera, between the ceiling and the roof, where he had taken refuge.

To go back to the engineer who used the aeroplane and the Parthenon as parallels: no comparison between the two is possible. The aeroplane has a mechanical beauty which is based on efficiency; but the beauty of the Parthenon must be of a different kind, because, as we have shown, the Doric temple was structurally an inefficient building. What is beauty? All Nature is beautiful, and no natural scene or object is ugly. The apple-tree in bloom hardly needs a poet to sing its praises, and the crocodile, though fearsome, is really found to be a very decorative beast when drawn. The beauty of the Doric temple must depend on the subtle way each part of it bears some definite proportion to the whole, and as the character of the building seems to have precluded the architects from experiment, they were able to concentrate their energies on making the one type as beautiful as possible in all its details.

Vitruvius says that "Proportion is that agreeable harmony between the several parts of a building, which is the result of a just and regular agreement of them with each other; the height to the width, this to the length, and each of these to the whole." He points out that proportion is as necessary to the beauty of a building as it is to the human figure. To-day we have not the faintest idea of the importance which these old architects attached to proportion. Vitruvius goes on to measure up the human figure and says that—

from the chin to the top of the forehead should equal one-tenth of the height of the body;

" " crown of the head should equal one-eighth of the height of the body;

from the upper part of the breast to the roots of the hair should equal one-sixth of the height of the body ;

„ „ „ breast to the crown of the head should equal one-fourth of the height of the body ;

the length of the foot should equal one-sixth of the height of the body ;

„ „ forearm should equal one-fourth of the height of the body ;

and so on. As well, that " The navel is naturally placed in the centre of the human body, and, if in a man lying with his face upward, and his hands and feet extended, from his navel as the centre, a circle be described, it will touch his fingers and toes."

Vitruvius suggests that the sturdier Doric column was founded on the proportions of a man's figure, and the slenderer Ionic on that of the woman's (see p. 56).

In another place Vitruvius points out how useful it is for the architect to know something about octaves, fourths, and fifths, because " music assists him in the use of harmonic and mathematical proportion."

All this sounds very annoying to us moderns. We like to keep things in nice idea-tight compartments, and we don't want anybody to show us how to do lifeless archi-ture. Not so the Greek : he gathered his inspiration from the whole book of Nature, and every manifestation of the spirit fired him. Certainly Vitruvius' recom-mendation, that the artist should study and draw the human figure, is a very sound one, as any student will find when he first confronts it in the " life " room of an art school, armed with nothing better than pencil and paper. If you are drawing an old building, or a gnarled tree, a few odd bumps don't make very much difference—with the human figure they do.

There can be no finer task for boys and girls than to try to discover this unsolved Greek secret of harmony and proportion.

Greek temples have been measured and photographed until their smallest details are known. During the Greek revival, which started with the publication, in 1762, by Stuart and Revett, of their book on the Antiquities of Athens, we tried what could be done by copying, and it did not amount to very much.

All of us will have seen Greek Doric caps in modern buildings, as Fig. 16, cut in stone, or moulded in plaster, technically all right, yet entirely wrong in spirit, as we find when we go to Greece, and see one of the originals set up against the background of a blue sky. No progress can be made by copying. It is the mumbling in a dead language of what is still a living art.

This Greek spirit of harmony and proportion is at once recognisable when seen. There is a good tale told of a Yorkshireman who went to Athens. He was a contractor, and had spent his life creating that wilderness of horror which we call Industrial England. In the evening of his days he thought he would travel, and so found himself on the Acropolis of Athens—and remember, he was an honest man, and would have described himself as a good "tradesman." He had built soundly, but without any sense of harmony and proportion, and now, quite suddenly, he was confronted with a masterpiece. Round and round the Parthenon he tramped, discovering fresh beauties every minute, and becoming more and more enraged, until at last his wrath flamed out and he cried, "Why was I not told about this before?" Or again, take the experiences of E. F. Benson, recounted in "As We Were." He, too, went to Athens, and wrote, "What an enlightenment was there." His approach had been by that "arid valley of education," which expunged "all human interest

FIG. 17.—Temple of Zeus Olympius, Girgenti, Sicily.
(House of the Giants.)

(*After Koldewey.*)

FIG. 18.—Temple of Poseidon, Pæstum, S. Italy.

and beauty from a subject which is instinct with humanity and loveliness."

To return to our temples. Syracuse, in Sicily, was one of the great Dorian colonies. A temple to Apollo, and the Olympium, were built there in the sixth century B.C., and a later one of the fifth century is now the Cathedral Church. It is an extraordinary experience to go into this Christian church and find Doric columns and caps, and then think that when they were newly cut it was Athene who was worshipped in the building.

At Selinus in Sicily there were no less than six temples, but all are in ruins. These were built in limestone, which was covered with a very fine stucco to take painted decorations, and by this time all the walling was of stone, and the sun-dried bricks were no longer used.

There are more temples at Acragas (Agrigentum or Girgenti) on the south coast of Sicily. When we were there we came across an American lady, seated on the steps of one, in an attitude of despair. She complained, "I'm tired of it, temple after temple, and all exactly alike." The lady was right and yet wrong. There are quite a lot of temples at Girgenti, but they are not all alike, though perhaps they do look so at first sight.

The town in the sixth century B.C. must have been a very important place. It stands back now about 2½ miles from the sea, on a raised table-land, bounded on the east by the River Acragas, and on the west by the Hypsa. The walls of the ancient city were 10 miles in circumference. The Acropolis, which is now the modern city, was at the northern extremity, and here was a temple, which, like the one at Syracuse, has been incorporated into a Christian church.

We are more concerned with the range of temples which was built on the southern boundary of the city looking towards the sea. At the eastern end is the Temple of Hera Laconia. Then moving west we come to the temples of Concord, Herakles, Zeus Olympius, Castor and Pollux, and Hephæstos. If we think of these temples, as they must have been at one time, decorated with glowing colours, and set on the top of the city wall hewn out of the rocky face of the hill on which they stood, with broad terraces, and flights of steps leading up to the temples, and adorned with the greenery of trees, and fine statues, we may be able to gain some faint idea of the beauties of Archaic Greece, and the splendid vision of her builders.

We have selected one of the southern temples, Zeus Olympius, for the subject of our illustration, Fig. 17. If by any chance the American lady comes across this book, we hope it will convince her that Greek temples are not all alike. The first thing to be noted is its great size. It stood on a platform, or stylobate, measuring 173 ft. by 361 ft. Imagine seven Doric columns set up at each end of this, and fourteen on each of the sides, and you will be able to form some idea of the scale of the building. The columns are not free standing as at Pæstum, Fig. 18, but have a wall filled in between them.

There would, of course, have been a pediment at each end of the building. Its technical description would be that it is heptastyle pseudo-peripteral (see Fig. 14). This only means that it had seven columns at each end, and that its peristyle, or colonnaded walk, was a false one, because it was blocked by the walls between the columns. These walls may have been necessary to support the entablature over, and here it is that we come to the tremendous figures which have given the temple its name of the House of the Giants. The figures are now broken and scattered on the ground. One has been roughly reconstructed and found to be 27 ft. in height. Many suggestions have been made as to their position in the building, and the most reasonable one seems to be that they acted as supports, as shown in

FIG. 19.—Temple of Artemis Aphaia, Ægina, Greece.
(*From a Photo by* MISS M. C. BENNETT.)

Fig. 20.—Heracles and a Dying Trojan.
(Sculptures from the Temple at Ægina, Greece.)
(in the Glyptothek, Munich.)

Fig. 17. Atlantes is the Greek term for male figures used in this way, and Caryatidæ for female ones. It is extraordinary on the site, when the guide points to a huge fragment of stone, and says, " There, you see, is a nose " ; and you think, " No, quite impossible," until you realise that a nose to fit a man 27 ft. high would be an enormous organ. We shall see later how the Greeks used figures at Delphi and Athens in this way.

Please note the relation of an ordinary man's figure to the scale of the building in Fig. 17. The columns are on such an enormous scale that a man's back fits quite comfortably into one of the flutings.

There was another Greek colony at Pæstum, in southern Italy (on the instep of the foot), and here there are two early temples, and one later (about 460 B.C.), dedicated to Poseidon, which is so well preserved that it is about the best illustration one can have of the Doric temple. (See Fig. 18 ; in plan it follows No. 3, Fig. 14.) Some idea of its size can be gained when you know that the diameter of the columns is 6 ft. 9½ in.

This temple will help us to understand another at Ægina, an island to the south of Salamis, as Fig. 19. This was dedicated to Artemis Aphaia, and dates from about 480 B.C. Its plan is shown in No. 3, Fig. 14. It is famous because of the wonderful sculptures of fighting Greeks and Trojans which once graced its pediments. The originals of these are in the Glyptothek, Munich. Our drawing, Fig. 21, shows how the sculptures were placed in the pediment. Fig. 20 is a photograph of two of the figures to a larger scale. We hope that boys and girls will pay great attention to Greek sculpture of this period and not dismiss it as Archaic. So far as we are concerned, it makes an especial appeal. It is so thoroughly architectural ; so cut and carved ; it fits its place so well ; the draperies do not flutter in the wind ; it has not yet come

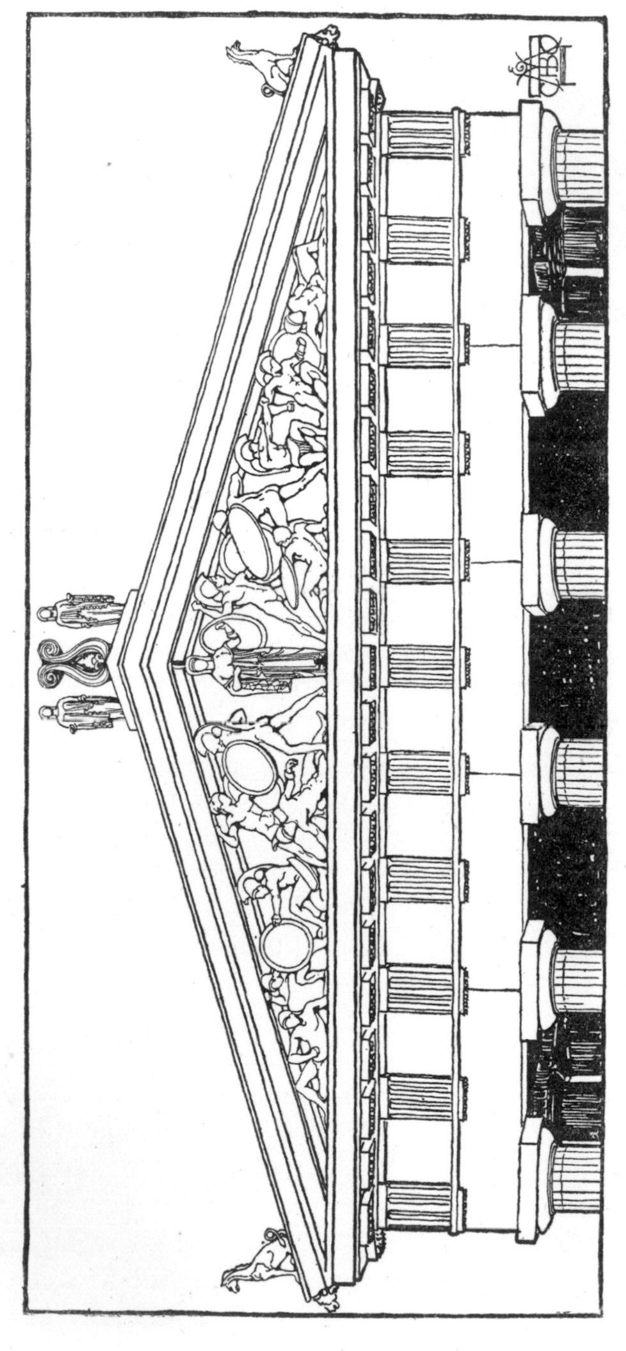

Fig. 21.—The W. Pediment of the Temple of Ægina (about 480 B.C.).

FIG. 22.—Lion's Head, from Doric Temple at Himera, Sicily.

(Drawing from Photograph published in "The Illustrated London News," by courtesy of Signor P. Marconi, Director of the National Museum, Palermo.)

to life and yet it is full of life. It is serene. "Summer" and "Winter" (Figs. 29 and 30) from the Ludovisi Throne, in the Museo Delle Terme, in Rome, are surely two of the most beautiful figure compositions made by man.

The lion's head, as Fig. 22, is a superb example of architectural sculpture. It formed part of the temple at Himera, built about 480 B.C., and destroyed by the Carthaginians in 409. The ruins were excavated in 1929 by the Italian Government. Forty of these lions' heads were found. They are now in the museum at Palermo.

Archaic Ionic

Just as we find the best examples of the early Doric temples in the Dorian colonies, so we must go to Ionia in Asia Minor for the early Ionic temples. If Syracuse was the most important Dorian colony, then Ephesus and Miletus led the way in Ionia.

Fig. 23 shows that the Ionic Order was very different to the Doric. Vitruvius says the Ionian architects "used the female figure as the standard," and made their columns eight times the diameter in height, and placed a base under it, like a shoe, and added volutes to the capital, like graceful, curling hair, and sunk channels on the shaft, as the folds on a matron's garment.

Perhaps the most celebrated archaic Ionic temple was that at Ephesus, dedicated to Artemis (Diana of the Ephesians).

We expect that boys and girls of to-day are more knowledgeable than we were; so far as we can remember, it never occurred to us, nor do we think it was suggested, that the Bible has a very interesting archæological background. We read fine-sounding names like Galatians and Ephesians, but hardly connected them with people, or pinned their names on the map.

Now St Paul must have known nearly all the places of which Herodotus wrote. In the *Acts*, chapter xix., we find that Paul "having passed through the upper coast came to Ephesus." It was during this visit that a silversmith named Demetrius, who made silver shrines for Diana, called together his fellow-craftsmen, and pointed out to them that Paul's preaching would turn away people from the worship of the great goddess, and they would find their occupation gone. "And when they heard these sayings, they were full of wrath, and cried out, saying, Great is Diana of the Ephesians."

The temple Paul knew was the later one, built after the fire, in 356 B.C., which destroyed the one we are now going to describe. This was dedicated to Artemis, who was the same goddess as the Roman Diana. Crœsus assisted in building this, before his overthrow by Cyrus in 546 B.C. His name is actually cut on a base from the temple in the Ephesus room at the British Museum. It was a vast building, the top of the platform measuring 180 ft. by 360 ft., as in Fig. 24. The cella, with its front and back porch, was surrounded by a double row of columns. The technical term for a double peristyle is dipteral. There were eight columns across the main façade (octastyle) and nine in the rear (enneastyle), and

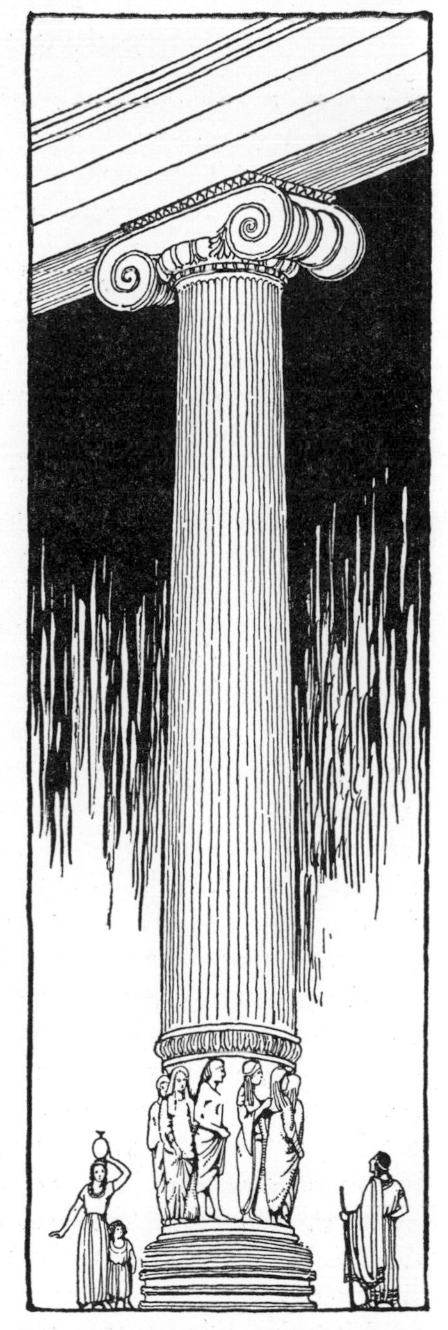

FIG. 23.—Reconstruction of the Ionic Order of the Archaic Temple at Ephesus.

there were twenty-one along the sides. Herodotus tells us that Crœsus gave golden heifers as an offering, and most of the columns. These columns were of unusual character. Ionic columns had moulded bases, unlike the Doric, which sprang directly off the stylobate without any base. Then above the base mould at Ephesus the lower drums of the columns themselves were sculptured with figures, and one of these drums, reconstructed from fragments, can be seen in the Ephesus room at the British Museum. The Ionic columns were more slender, eight or nine diameters high to the Doric four or five. There are, as well, at the British Museum, two of the Ionic capitals from Ephesus. One of these is shown in Fig. 23, and it should be noted how oblong it is in shape, and not square, as in the later Ionic caps. It probably, like the Doric, started life as a long pad of wood, cantilevered over each side of the column to pick up the weight of the architrave, and then to make it pretty the carpenter cut a spiral on each end, and this became the Ionic cap. The Ionic architrave is triply divided into three faces, and it is thought that this started as three wooden beams, each projected a little forward. The Ionic cornice was decorated with dentils, and these are thought to have been the ends of the cross-ceiling joists.

The general form and plan of the archaic Ionic temple was much like the Doric one. It was the details which varied. Beyond this we cannot say much, because there are no very complete ruins of an archaic Ionic temple, nothing as complete as the wonderful Doric ruins of the temple of Poseidon. Fig. 24, reproduced from a drawing by A. E. Henderson, who was the architect to the excavations at Ephesus, gives the best idea we have of an archaic Ionic temple.

Vitruvius tells us how the marble for the temple was discovered by a shepherd. During a fight between two

FIG. 24.—Reconstruction of the Archaic Temple at Ephesus, Asia Minor.

(*From the Drawing by* Mr A. E. HENDERSON, F.S.A., F.R.I.B.A., Architect to the EXCAVATIONS at Ephesus.)

FIG. 25.—The Siphnian Treasury, Delphi, Greece.

(From the Reconstruction in the Museum at Delphi.)

rams of his flock, the horns of one, glancing against a rock, broke off a splinter, which showed that it was marble. We are given as well details of the troubles which the architects of the temple, Chersiphron and Metagenes, had in transporting the marble from the quarries to the site. Finally, they found a solution by fixing it up as a gigantic garden roller, or, as Vitruvius says, "the rolling stone used for smoothing the walks in palæstræ (gymnasia)."

If there is no very complete archaic Ionic temple, there is a very valuable reconstruction, in the Delphi Museum, of a treasury built at Delphi by the Siphnians (Fig. 25). Siphnos is an island in the Cyclades. These treasuries were built in the form of small temples, at the great shrine, as the headquarters for the people sent to Delphi during the festivals. This Siphnian treasury is Ionic in character, of the *in antis* type, as No. 1, Fig. 14. It has caryatidæ (or maidens, as the Greeks first called them) instead of Ionic columns. The treasury was built about 525 B.C., of marble, brilliantly coloured, so that it is very interesting as a forerunner of the Erectheum built on the Acropolis at Athens.

We shall have to wait till the next volume to be able to illustrate the wonderful little Ionic Temple of the Wingless Victory at Athens, and the Erectheum where the Ionic style culminated.

Meanwhile there are some very wonderful archaic Ionic sculptures to give us joy, and here we might pay some more detailed attention to the Ionian and the Dorian sculptors, whose work we have already illustrated. We are apt to take Greek sculpture for granted, and not to realise what a miracle it was. These archaic sculptures date from about the middle of the sixth century B.C., and the work of Phidias at the Parthenon was about a hundred years later. Neither before, nor after, has there been any sculpture to compare with theirs—in fact, the greatest compliment a sculptor of any period can be paid, is to be told that his work has a Greek quality.

It is worth while paying a visit to the British Museum to test this. If we go to the Egyptian gallery first, we shall find figures there which are both dexterous and decorative, but animals' heads are grafted on to human bodies, and the work is repellent. The people shown are of a poor physical type. There was no inspiration for Greece here.

If we go to the Assyrian gallery, there are sculptures of 884-860 B.C. Here, again, we find great technical accomplishment and decorative value, but all are disfigured by cruelty. Animals are shown in traps waiting to be loosed and shot through with arrows; men are impaled, and captives toil in transporting colossal figures. Here, again, there was no inspiration for Greece, and we can pass on to the Archaic room, where we shall find the sculptures we have illustrated in Figs. 3 to 10, and so through to the Parthenon sculptures in the Elgin room. As soon as we enter the Greek rooms we are conscious of some great difference.

The Egyptian sculptors sought perhaps to render some individual immortal. The Assyrians satisfied the pride of kings. The Greeks seem to have been able to obtain an abstraction of beauty which was not concerned with the individual at all, and, lacking all self-consciousness, the individuals are as serene and beautiful as gods. How were they able to do this? There are certain Greek characteristics which must be borne in mind. They had tremendously inquiring minds, and took nothing for granted. We shall write later of Thales of Miletus, an Ionian, and the first of the philosophers, or lovers of knowledge for its own sake. The early philosophers asked themselves, "What is this world in which we live?" In the most amazing way to us, they mixed their philosophy up with mathematics, and sought for some combination of numbers which would give them a formula to solve the puzzle.

We may be sure that the artists followed suit, and they would have been concerned with Beauty. Perhaps the philosophers helped the artists, and passed on to them their ideas of rhythm, harmony, and proportion. The Greeks were great talkers, and there must have been tremendous discussions as to What is Beauty? and their analytical minds would have taken them to Nature, which is the ultimate source of inspiration for all artists. They probably not only feasted their eyes on the beauty of natural forms and colour, but sought for clues as to the actual mystery and process of creation. They watched how in the autumn the flowers fade, the seeds ripen, the leaves wither, the plants die and sleep through the winter. The illusion of death passes because the spring soon comes with the reality of life. This is the time for miracles. Even before the buds come the twigs are coloured by the rising sap, the greyness of the cold passes into tender greens, the air is full of fragrance, and in one rush of blossom the spring is here. Now man can understand the autumn, but spring is beyond his comprehension: he can only feel that if one is like death, the other is obviously the miracle of life. It seems to him that the gods are at work, and the divinity in him is stirred. He, too, wishes to create, and so he takes stone or marble, and builds and carves; brushes, and paints; his lyre, and sings; pen, and writes—and in doing so he expresses himself most surely, and stands revealed. He succeeds if, as in the case of the Greeks, the gods have been very good to him, and he understands in some measure the message of spring.

To return to the Archaic sculptures.

Figs. 3 to 10 are of a set of lovely bas-reliefs in the

FIG. 26.—Archaic Bronze, 550 B.C.
(*British Museum.*)

Archaic room at the British Museum. On quite a large scale, the actual sizes are noted on the drawings, the figures are cut in low relief, and, being very old and faded, do not at first sight, perhaps, seem quite so beautiful as they do after some study. The best way to do this is, of course, to make drawings yourselves; the drawing may not be a great success, but the concentrated attention which was necessary for its making, will discover the beauties of the sculpture for you. What could be more engaging than the fighting cocks, and they are as decorative as a Japanese

Fig. 27.—Archaic Female Figure.

(*Acropolis Museum, Athens.*)

Fig. 28.—The Charioteer.

(*Museum at Delphi.*)

FIG. 29.—Summer.

FIG. 30.—Winter.

(In the Museo Delle Terme, Rome.)

drawing. The line of the leopard or lioness, in Fig. 7, is superb, and the spring of the lion is full of life.

The sculptors were equally happy when working in bronze.

There is the small equestrian bronze, as Fig. 26, which dates from about 550 B.C. Do not dismiss this as amusingly archaic, go to the Bronze room at the British Museum, and study it very carefully. Only a few inches high, it seems to us worthy to rank with its larger brother, the statue of Colleoni, by Verrocchio, in Venice. All down the centuries, artists have struggled with this problem of man and horse together, and their successes can be counted on the fingers of one hand. This little archaic bronze is one of them. It is alive, and the horse, though at rest, is full of movement.

The charming little archaic lady, Fig. 49, in the British Museum, is inlaid with silver, and has small diamonds for the pupils of the eyes. It is probably of a later date.

Houses

Having dealt with the temples or houses of the gods, and their adornments, we can pass on to the homes of men, and here we are at once in difficulties, because there are so few remains of the early types. From the earliest times there seem to have been two types, a northern and a southern, and of these the southern was much more advanced. This from the earliest times was a rectangular building, with a flat terraced roof made of logs, covered with a layer of clay. An example of the New Stone Age has been found at Magasa, in Crete. Here, even before 1700 B.C., we find it developed into a town house, with two or even three storeys. Fig. 31 illustrates one of these, and is a reconstruction from one of the faience plaques, showing house fronts discovered at Cnossos. The bases of the walls were rubble masonry, and on these timber framing was erected, filled in with sun-dried brick,

FIG. 31.—Minoan House.

which was plastered, and in all probability gaily decorated with colours. Generally at the ground-floor level there was only the door from the street. The windows over are quite modern in appearance, divided up with mullions and transoms. The small projection on the top obviously screened a staircase up to the roof. Staircases offered no difficulty to the Minoan architects (see Fig. 9, Vol. I., in this Series).

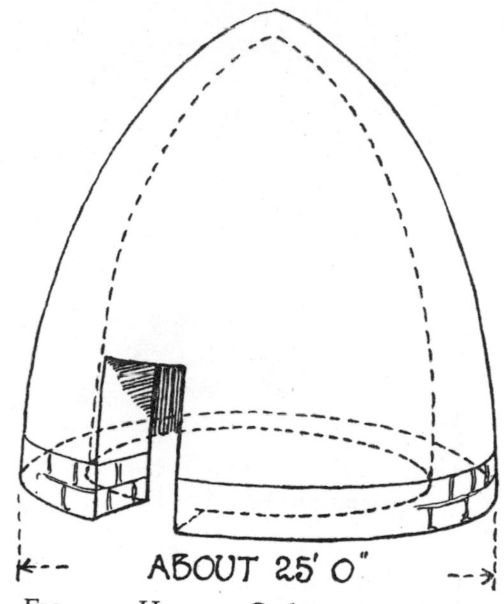

FIG. 32.—House at Orchomenus, Bœotia, Greece.

The northern type of house seems to have developed from the circular hut, formed by leaning saplings against a central post with a covering of thatch, until the shape was like that of the bell-tent. This must be nearly as old as man himself. We saw in "Everyday Life," Vol. I., how in the Old Stone Age the Aurignac and La Madeleine drawings suggested this hut form. Again, in "Everyday Life," Vol. II., in the New Stone Age in England, we found the same circular hut, with its conical roof, but vertical walls had been added under to give more height inside. This circular hut was the forerunner of the beehive domed house. This type was built first of wattle and daub, and then of sun-dried bricks, as Fig. 32. Ruins of this type have been found at Orchomenus, in Bœotia, and it must have been the inspiration for the wonderful

FIG. 33.—Reconstruction Based on Hut Urn from the Island of Melos.

Tomb of Agamemnon at Mycenæ, which we illustrated in Figs. 52 to 53, Vol. I. This was a beehive house, only built underground as befitting a home for the dead.

Now we come to a remarkable terracotta urn, found in the island of Melos (the original is in the Munich Museum). The urn is remarkable because it shows the way that man goes to work. He needed a larger type of house than the single hut, and obtained it by placing seven huts together so that they enclosed a courtyard, the open end of which was closed by a wall with a gate and porch (Fig. 33). Looking back, it seems a childish conception, but the man who did it was an architectural hero—he had planned the first courtyard—by happy accident. By the way, this must be remembered. As historians you must be prepared to go back, and then look forward with the people. In this way you can share their triumphs. To look back, or look down, from your superior knowledge is fatal.

This type of plan must have proved rather inconvenient, and wasteful of material and difficult to roof. Still, the architects had discovered that it was possible to group parts into a whole. The next step seems to have been a type of plan, as Fig. 34, of the apsidal house at Korakou, Corinth, where the walls between the huts have been done away with and the sides straightened. Here the plan appears to have been based on two and a half huts.

Half a hut became the apse at the back, used as a bed-room (*thalamus*); the hall occupied one and a half huts; the porch (*prodomus*) another half-hut, squared up for convenience. This offered a much less difficult roofing problem, and the thatch could then be laid in two plain slopes. The next step was the fully developed hall plan of the Megaron at Tiryns, which was illustrated in Fig. 57, Vol. I.

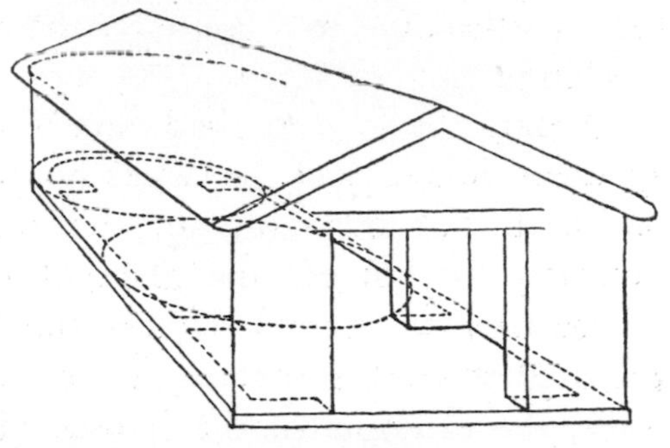

FIG. 34.—Apsidal House at Korakou, Corinth.

The small terra-cotta model of a house found in an eighth-century B.C. burial at Argos, which we used as Fig. 1, Vol. I., to illustrate the swineherd's house, is evidently a descendant of the apsidal house at Korakou, and then the evidence becomes scanty.

One reason for this was that the Greeks did not pay much attention to their houses. Their climate allowed them to live out of doors, and as there was nothing they enjoyed more than good talk, they passed a lot of their time in the agora, or market-place, where they could be sure of meeting their fellow-men. Their houses were used for feeding and sleeping. Demosthenes, in one of his orations, said: "The great men of old built splendid edifices for the use of the State, and set up noble works of art which later ages can never match. But in private life they were severe and simple, and the dwelling of an Aristides or a Miltiades was no more sumptuous than that of an ordinary Athenian citizen." It is to their credit, then, that they paid more attention to building the Parthenon to house Athene than their own dwellings.

Again, the climate had something to do with the apparent simplicity of the Greek house. It looked inwards on itself, not outwards on the world, because it was necessary to shut out the glare of the sun and the dust of the narrow streets. Unless the Greek builders were prepared to plaster meaningless ornament on the outside walls, the exteriors of the houses of necessity had to be very simple.

As to the actual detail of the houses of the fifth century B.C., the only example we know are the remains of one at Dystus in Eubœa. Before we start on the details of the houses, it may be as well to consult Vitruvius, because his explanations of Greek houses will help us. He said the Greeks did not have an atrium, meaning, not a complete court, with colonnaded walks roofed over and open in the centre. The entrance passage (of no great breadth) from the entrance gate had the stable on one side and porters' rooms on the other, next the inner gate. From this one enters into the Peristylium, with a portico on three sides. " On that side facing the south are two antæ, at a considerable distance apart, which carry beams, and the recess behind them is equal to one-third less than their distance from each other." This was the porch (*pronaos*). This led to the house-place, or living-room (*œcus*), where the mistress sat with the spinsters. To the right and left of this porch were two bedchambers (*thalamus* and *antithalamus*). Round the porticos are dining-rooms (*triclinia*) for common use, the bedchambers and other apartments for the family.

Though Vitruvius' description must apply to later Greek houses, we can still find the various parts in Fig. 35 of the (fifth century) house at Dystus: 1 was the entrance, and 2 appears to be the porters' room. Apparently horses

FIG. 35.—Plan and Reconstruction of House at Dystus, Eubœa, Greece.

were not kept, but if they had been, the stable would have been on the right-hand side of the entrance passage. According to the fourth book of the "Odyssey," the chariot, which was a very light affair, was kept "tilted up against the shining walls of the entry." 3 was the court or peristylium; 4 was the hall, or house-place; 5 the bedchambers. The other rooms were used for general family purposes—one would have been the kitchen. At 6 was the exedra, or recess, where people could sit out in the summer. There may have been an upper floor for the women, approached by a staircase, at 7. We saw in Vol. I. how Penelope had an upper chamber that she retired to when the suitors in the hall were a nuisance.

In Vol. III. we shall be able to give rather fuller details of the Greek house.

CHAPTER III.—LIFE INSIDE THE HOUSE

The sixth-century Greek architect, like the English one in the Middle Ages, had a very much simpler task than his successors of to-day. In the Greek and mediæval houses one had to provide a hall, and various other rooms which had traditional positions—one put these in their places, and everybody was happy and satisfied. If one had to pass across one room to get to another, nobody was worried, or talked about privacy being disturbed; in the same way, one might have to cross a courtyard.

Not quite so much to-day, but most certainly in the nineteenth century, the architect was asked to design houses with separate access to each room, which had to have a door so that its inhabitants could lock themselves in—as if they were forgers. The servants had to be removed as far away as possible, and "shut off." To surprise a housemaid at her task was unthinkable, and to see the cook peeling potatoes would have disturbed the entire household.

We must forget all this when considering the life which was led in such a simple house as the one at Dystus (Fig. 35). It probably housed a larger family than it would have done to-day. We mean there may have been grandparents, an uncle and aunt perhaps, and not just father, mother, and children. There would not have been more privacy than was obtainable in our own Penshurst of 1341. The two bedchambers must have been for the family—the maids and children would have gone upstairs to the rooms over the exedra, and here the women may have retired when the menfolk were entertaining their friends. The slaves and any other folk would have slept in any odd corner—after all, it is not so long ago that the draper's apprentice slept under his master's shop counter, and probably found it quite cosy.

Vitruvius gives us one indication of the use of the hall, when he says that here " the mistress of the family sits with the spinsters." The married women did the weaving, and their daughters the spinning—hence spinster for an unmarried woman. However, the Greek climate is so pleasant that the hall door would have been open most of the time, and a great deal of the work done in the open court, or under the exedra—here we may be sure that vine and fig trees added colour to the scene.

Food

From the point of view of the housewife, the most constant need of man has always been his food, and her main occupation has been to " feed the brute." Here Vitruvius helps us again. Talking of some of the later and larger houses, he says that separate apartments were provided for guests, like the " lodgings " in an Elizabethan house, and that the guests were provided " with poultry, eggs, herbs, fruit, and other produce of the country." This seems to have been the bill of fare for the Greek in late Archaic or Classical times. They were not mighty eaters of meat, like the heroes of the Trojan War. This in a way is an indication of the northern extraction of the latter. Meat, after all, was not needed in a climate like that of Greece, or only occasionally, when a beast had been sacrificed to a god. Then, after the proper portions had been offered on the altar, the family feasted on the remainder.

In some late fourth-century houses at Priene, near Miletus, in Asia Minor, hearths were found in a central position in some of the halls, like that in the Megaron in Tiryns, which we illustrated as Fig. 60 in Vol. I. Here, perhaps, slices of meat were grilled before the fire, or black puddings, like the one Odysseus won by beating Arnæus. Cooking utensils were found in some cases in the porches outside the halls at Priene, where they would have been close at hand for use in the hall. One of the smaller rooms in the house at Dystus (Fig. 35) may have been used as a kitchen, for the preparation of vegetable dishes. All that was necessary was a raised hearth, like the one found at the Roman Pompeii, which we illustrated in "Everyday Life," Vol. III. On this hearth small charcoal fires were made, and the food stewed over them in saucepans, or fried in olive oil.

Bread seems to have been baked in a portable pottery oven. There is a model of one in the Greek and Roman Life room at the British Museum. It would have been simple to make a wood fire in one of these, and then rake the ashes to one side and imprison the heat to bake the bread by putting on a lid. It is the same principle as the cooking pit of the New Stone Age and the brick oven of old farm houses. We must not be superior and expect too much in the Greek house. Take Little Wenham Hall (Fig. 55, "E.T.," I.), near Ipswich, built in England in the thirteenth century A.D. The accommodation there consisted of a hall and chapel, a room for the lord, and a store-room. The kitchen must have been outside the house, and all food had to be carried in.

In one respect the people who lived in the house at Dystus were fortunate; they had a well in their courtyard from which they could draw water. Even to-day, when one is building a house in the country, water is the first thing to be settled. Unless one has a water main in the road, one must sink a well, or tap a spring. If one cannot find water, one cannot build. So it must have been in Archaic Greece.

From the fact that the black-figure vase painters frequently drew women going to the fountains, we can assume that this was the general source of supply. The builders of the city would have chosen a site where there was a good spring, and then conducted the water by pipes to a fountain in the market-place, where it could be

FIG. 36.—The Fountain.

(From a Black-figure Vase in the British Museum.)

discharged through lions' heads, so that the women could fill their jugs. Judged from the vase drawings, these fountains were very pleasant architectural compositions; we have restored one in Fig. 36.

The women probably enjoyed going to the fountain. Once, when we were in Rome, the water supply to the houses failed, so the women had to go to the public fountains, as in the old days—and they appeared to enjoy it. Their gossip sounded like the twitterings of the starlings returning to their home in the porch of the British Museum on a winter evening.

Pottery

From kitchens, cooking and water supply, we pass naturally enough to pots and pans. We must remember that pottery is one of the oldest arts, and has been practised here in England since the New Stone Age. Pottery is like glass-blowing—the maker has only his hands and a few simple tools, but a material which lends itself very readily to shaping. It is a dangerous craft. In the hands of the vulgarian horrors are produced, but to the artist there are tremendous possibilities. Shape must be considered, and our illustrations will show how beautiful and varied the shapes can be. Then pottery has to be handled, so the quality of the surface should be pleasant; one doesn't want to set one's fingers on edge. The old potters were very good, and considered their surfaces carefully. Pottery lends itself to decoration, and every conceivable type has been used. This should be noted. The Minoans, who were wonderful potters, and could draw the figure admirably, did not use it to decorate their vases. The Greeks did, and so their vases have become almost of as much importance as historical documents in showing the feats of the heroes and the details of everyday life. Then pottery is nearly indestructible, and the archæologist uses the potsherd to date the strata through which he digs.

In these notes the consequences of two catastrophic occurrences are well shown—the fall of Cnossus, and the Dorian Invasion of Greece. After each, man shows himself as a busy little insect. He is like an ant whose hill has been disturbed. He gets to work as soon as possible to repair the damage, and produces more pots—not so good as the old ones, perhaps, but gradually improving all the while. So the tale of an art can be shown as cemented by courage.

Like everything else, the Greek vases have a long history behind them. Excavations in northern Greece (Bœotia, Phocis, and Thessaly) have unearthed richly painted vases, decorated with line ornament in red and white, which date from the New Stone Age, and what is curious is, that northern Greece appears to have been in advance of the south during this early period.

In the early Bronze Age this pottery gave way to coarse unpainted ware. At Hagia Marina, in Phocis, after the New Stone Age, they had a hand-made ware with a black or red glaze, and rectilinear ornaments. This was followed at Orchomenus by " Minyan " ware, of dark grey or yellow, turned on a wheel. Then there came what is known as Creto-Mycenæan, dating from the first late Minoan period, at the end of the Bronze Age. This must have been imported from Crete, and was found by Schliemann in the shaft graves at Mycenæ (of which we wrote in Vol. I., p. 88), in conjunction with the local Minyan ware.

It is obvious, then, that we must go back to Crete to discover the beginnings of Greek pottery. The New Stone Age pottery, found in northern Greece, was in advance of that found in Crete, probably because that period lasted longer in Thessaly. Crete seems to have become prosperous suddenly. By the middle Minoan period (2200-1600 B.C.)

FIG. 37.—Kamares Vase.

FIG. 38.—Late Minoan Vase.

they were making pottery with a good black glaze, and decorating it with many colours.

The Kamares ware (Fig. 37), from Cnossos and Phaistos, followed, and here both in shape and the decorations in white, red, and yellow on black, it is easy to see that the potters had made wonderful advances. It was exported to the Ægean Islands and Egypt.

This was followed by middle Minoan III. and late Minoan I., as Fig. 38, and now for a short period the potters revelled in a more naturalistic treatment, and employed seaweed and other marine plants, and cuttle-fish, among others, as decorative symbols. This would be about 1500 B.C. The genius who first thought of using the cuttle-fish must have been rather proud of it when applied to the pot.

In the second late Minoan times there was a return to a more rigid style of decoration, called now the Palace style, and then disaster fell on Crete, and the interest shifts to the mainland of Greece. We have come to the Achæan people of whom we wrote in Vol. I., and the work they did,

FIG. 39.—Late Mycenæan Vase.

called late Mycenæan, cannot compare with the Minoan work. Fig. 39 shows one of their vases, in yellowish clay decorated with red. After this came the Dorian Invasion, and the potters had to start again. It is now that we come to the start of Greek vases proper, and Fig. 40 shows one in the first Vase room at the British Museum, in the geometric style, 900-700 B.C. At the end of the period we come to the Dipylon ware, so called because very fine examples have been found in a cemetery near the Dipylon Gate in Athens. The decoration is geometric in character, and figures are introduced. Looking at these quaint figures is a good reminder of how knowledge can be lost. In the frescoes at Cnossos and Tiryns, and the sculpture of the Lion Gate at Mycenæ (Fig. 51, Vol. I.), great anatomical knowledge was displayed, and this had all been forgotten, and a beginning made again in these quaint little figures.

About the seventh century B.C. there were new developments. By this time the Greek colonies in Asia Minor were firmly established, and they served as a half-way house between the East and Greece. They collected oriental fabrics and metal ware, and traded them back to their homeland. Here they served as an inspiration to the potters, and the new style of pottery came to be called Corinthian, as Fig. 41, doubtless because Corinth was a great trading centre.

The decoration advances, and the palmette, or honeysuckle pattern, is employed, and well-drawn animals are painted in continuous bands, in black and purple on yellow backgrounds, the outlines being incised by lines scratched on the surface of the clay. In the later Corinthian vases the animals give way to the human figure. In the second Vase room at the British Museum there is a plate with a fine drawing on it of the fight between Hector and Menelaos.

Work like this prepared the way for the black-figure vases of the sixth century B.C.—so called, because the figure and ornaments were painted directly in a black varnish on to the orange-red clay of the background. Detail was given to the figures by incised lines; sometimes purple and white were added for the same purpose. These black-figure vases are contemporary with the Archaic architecture and sculpture, and have the same charm, and it is these which would have been used in the house at Dystus. Fig. 42 shows the design on the bottom of the cup of a kylix, at Munich, by Exekias. (See Fig. 43 for shape of kylix.) This is founded on the legend of Dionysus, the god of the vine, given in one of the Homeric Hymns. The god was once by the seaside when pirates who were sailing by spied him, and coming ashore seized, bound, and carried him to the ship, thinking to sell Dionysus as a slave. But his bonds fell away, and the pirates were afraid, and hoisted their sail, thinking that the god could not escape when they were at sea. But fragrant wine flowed through the ship, and a vine sprouted and twined round the mast; meanwhile the god was changed into a roaring lion, and a bear, and the pirates leapt overboard and were changed into dolphins; you can see them sporting round the ship in Fig. 42.

What could be more charming than this design? and think of the difficulty of decorating the spherical interior. But the tale is told and the kylix decorated. This is an interesting point; works of art fail if they lose their

FIG. 40.—"Geometric" Vase.
900–700 B.C.
(British Museum.)

FIG. 41.—Corinthian Vase.
(British Museum.)

FIG. 42.—Design in the Cup of a Black-figure Kylix.
(*Munich.*)

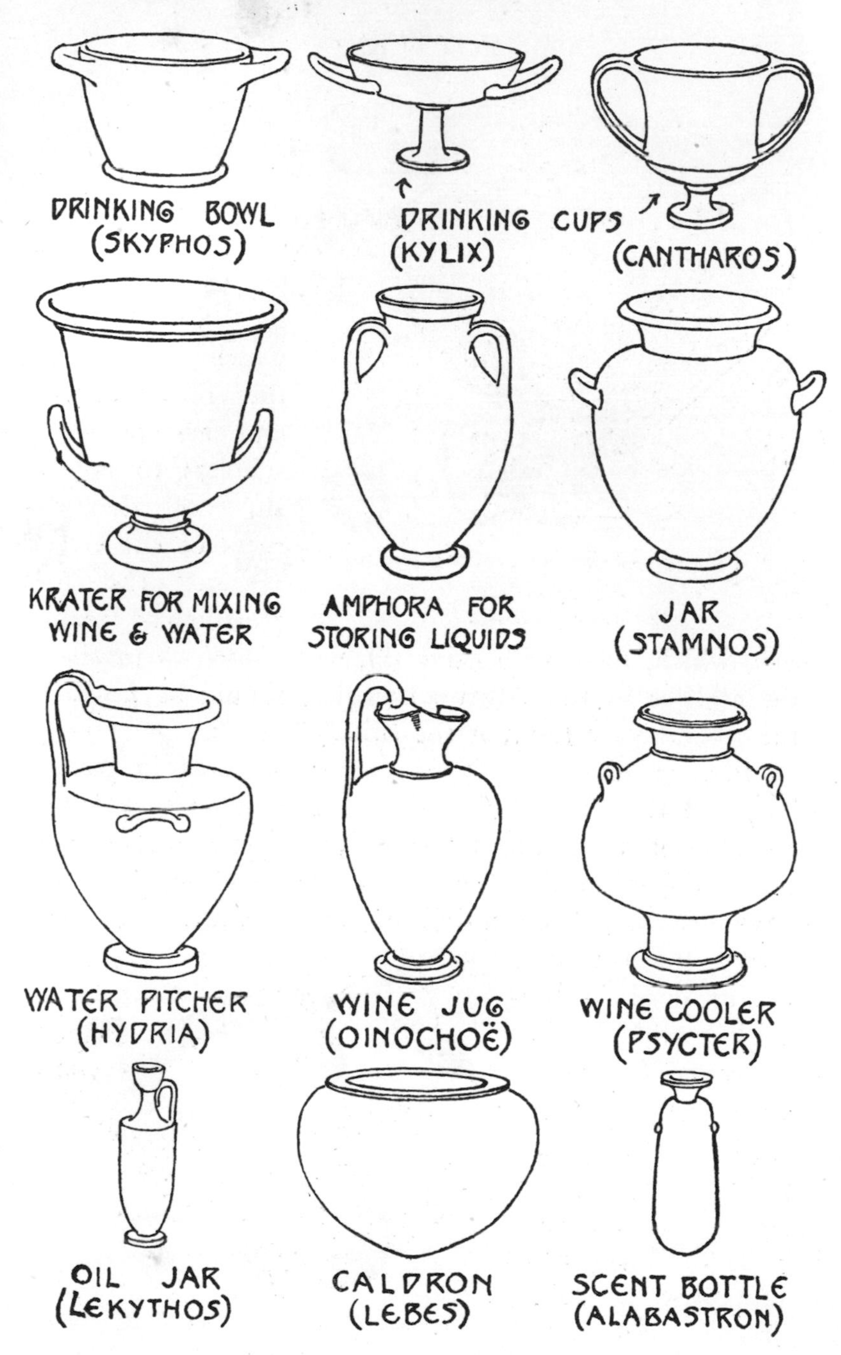

FIG. 43.—Types of Greek Vases.

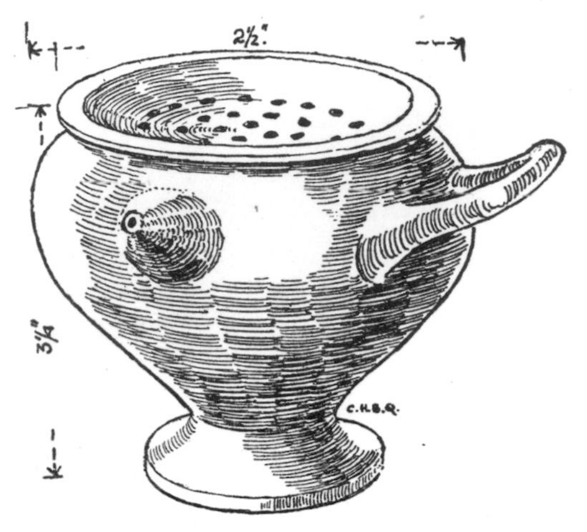

FIG. 44.—Athenian Feeding Bottle, about 500 B.C.
(British Museum.)

decorative value. Here it is that we think that the black-figure vases are sometimes better than the later red-figured ones which followed in the fifth century, and are held by scholars to be the supreme development of the Greek potter. The fine panathenaic amphoræ, which, filled with olive oil, were given as prizes to the athletes in the Athenian games, should be noted in the second Vase room at the British Museum.

Fig. 43 gives the types of Greek vases in general use, and their technical names. The fine pieces would have been used for table purposes, or to decorate the sitting-rooms. The vases we see in museums have generally been found in tombs, where they were placed for the use of the dead in the spirit world. Plain, undecorated ware was used for kitchen and storage purposes. The big jars (*pithoi*), with pointed ends, were supported by being driven into the earth.

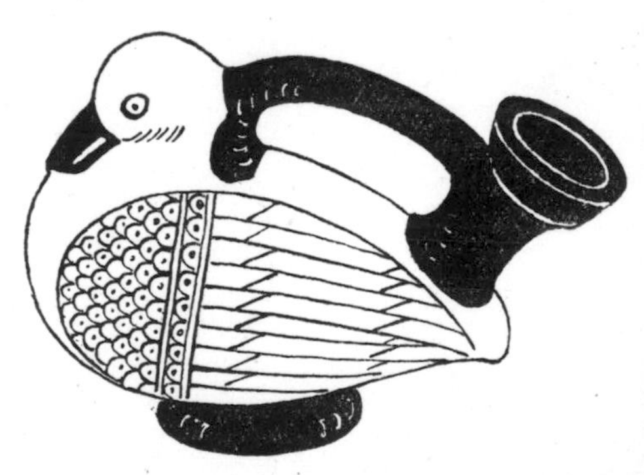

FIG. 45.—Oil Flask (*Askos*), Athenian Black Figure.
(British Museum.)

FIG. 46.—Patterns from Greek Vases.

FIG. 47.—The Dorian Chiton.

COSTUME

Having considered cooking, and pots and pans, we can now think about dress. If, of the three primary occupations, feeding comes easily first—one must eat to live—the second place must be given to dressing. We may be sure that the Greek woman, with a roof over her head, after she had fed her family, turned her attention to clothes. Here she was not so much worried as the English mother of to-day, by the number and complexity of the garments still required by her boys.

Taking her own garments first, she wove on her loom (illustrated in Fig. 40, Vol. I.) what we should call a dress-length, about 6 ft. wide by 11 ft. long. This she made into her principal garment, the chiton, without any cutting or waste of material; and this is a very important detail to note in the drawings. Herodotus has told us (p. 20) of the two types of chiton, the Dorian and Ionian. The Dorian was made very simply, by taking the length of material and folding over about a quarter of its width.

FIG. 48.—The Ionian Chiton.

It was then arranged and fastened on the shoulders by brooches, as at A, Fig. 47, and fell into the familiar folds as at B. In the earlier styles the open side was not sewn up, but it was secured by a girdle at the waist, and the material was pulled out and pouched over the girdle. The turned-over piece which hung down at back and front, looks, in some vase drawings, as if it was a separate tunic, but this is not the case. The later chitons were sewn up at the sides.

The Dorian chiton was fastened, at first, on the shoulders, by pins made of the leg bones of small animals, fibulæ, and later, when they came to be made of metal, with the disastrous results noted by Herodotus on p. 20, they were still called by the same name. Our safety-pin of to-day is a descendant of these bone pins.

The earliest garments were woven in fine wool, and here is a point to be noted by anyone who makes Greek dresses—they will look much " bunchier " than the vase drawings. Even a fine woollen material, like Viyella, does

Fig. 49.—Bronze Statuette.
(*British Museum.*)

not hang in quite the desired way, and we get our best results with crêpe-de-chine.

The Ionian chiton was introduced early in the sixth century. This was much more like a dress, and did not have the turned-over piece, so it was more economical so far as the material was concerned. The width was about 4 ft. 6 in., and the length twice the span of the arms, say 11 ft. The material was folded and sewn as C, Fig. 48, leaving holes for the head and arms, and it then fell into folds as D. Finely crinkled linen, like crape, was used, and sometimes muslin. The chiton was girdled and pouched. Sometimes the material was striped, and had fringes added. Saffron and red seem to have been favourite colours. Under the chiton the woman may have worn a little slip, and probably a broad belt to support the figure.

We may be sure there were varying fashions ; the vase

FIG. 50.—End of Sixth Century B.C. Athenian Fabric. Warrior Blowing Trumpet through Mouthpiece.
(*British Museum.*)

FIG. 51.—Hermes, Sixth Century. Black-figure Vase.
(*British Museum.*)

drawings show variations. In any case, woman has always wished to make herself look as nice as possible, and in so doing has set an example to her menfolk, and saved them from relapsing into a masculine barbarism. Her greatest opportunity in Greek times seems to have been in the use of the mantle, or himation. This, again, was a plain oblong, but of many sizes, and worn in varying ways. A small himation might be thrown over the shoulders and worn indoors on chilly days, and a larger one as a cloak when going outdoors. Sometimes they are shown under the left arm and over the right shoulder, or a fold might be drawn up as a head covering. They

FIG. 52.—Sixth Century B.C. Archer in Asiatic Costume Blowing Trumpet through Mouthpiece.
(*British Museum.*)

have pretty decorative borders, and are shown hanging in such cunning folds that it almost suggests the himation was sometimes pleated. These are well shown on the archaic bronze (Fig. 49, or Fig. 27) of one of the female archaic figures in the Acropolis Museum at Athens. These are irreverently known as the "Aunts," and were discovered in excavations on the Acropolis site. They were there when the Persians destroyed the Acropolis in 480 B.C. (p. 29), and afterwards must have just been shovelled into the ground to assist in building up a new level.

Women had various ways of doing their hair, and wore caps and veils. Our illustrations, which have all been made from black-figure vase drawings, show as many types as we have been able to find.

Indoors the Greeks do not seem to have worn shoes, and sometimes not out of doors.

When we come to man's costume, we find that the most important garment was a plain tunic, which could be short in the case of the peasant, or much longer where one had a draughty job, like the charioteer, as Fig. 28.

Sometimes the tunic was short and tight, and worn under the armour, as Fig. 50. Another useful garment for the working man was a short double apron, as Fig. 71. Men of rank appear to have worn white, and the peasants a natural wool colour. There were conical caps and useful high boots, as Fig. 51.

We may be quite sure that the next thing the Greek woman turned her attention to, after having fed and clothed her family, was the furnishing of the house.

Furniture

Here, again, we shall have to consult the vase paintings and sculptured monuments. The principal pieces seem to have been the couches used by the men to recline on when dining. The women did not use them in this way, but sat on a chair when taking their meals. The food was served and brought in on the light three-legged tables, one to each person, as Fig. 53. These were low enough to be pushed under the couches when not in use. The couches served as beds at night, and had a mattress supported by interlaced cords, or leather thongs stretched between the wooden frame. Fig. 54 shows a baby's cot from a black-figure vase. There were chairs and stools, and clothes were kept in chests, as they were in England until the beginning of the seventeenth century, and the other things were hung on nails in the wall. The houses would have looked rather bare to us, but they were undoubtedly labour-saving. There were many beautiful types of chairs —no less than three are shown on the Harpies' Tomb in the British Museum. This dates from about the middle of the sixth century B.C., so we are given admirable details of Ionian furniture of that period. The three chairs are seats of honour (*thronos*), and footstools were generally used with them. Fig. 55 has square-cut feet, with terminals

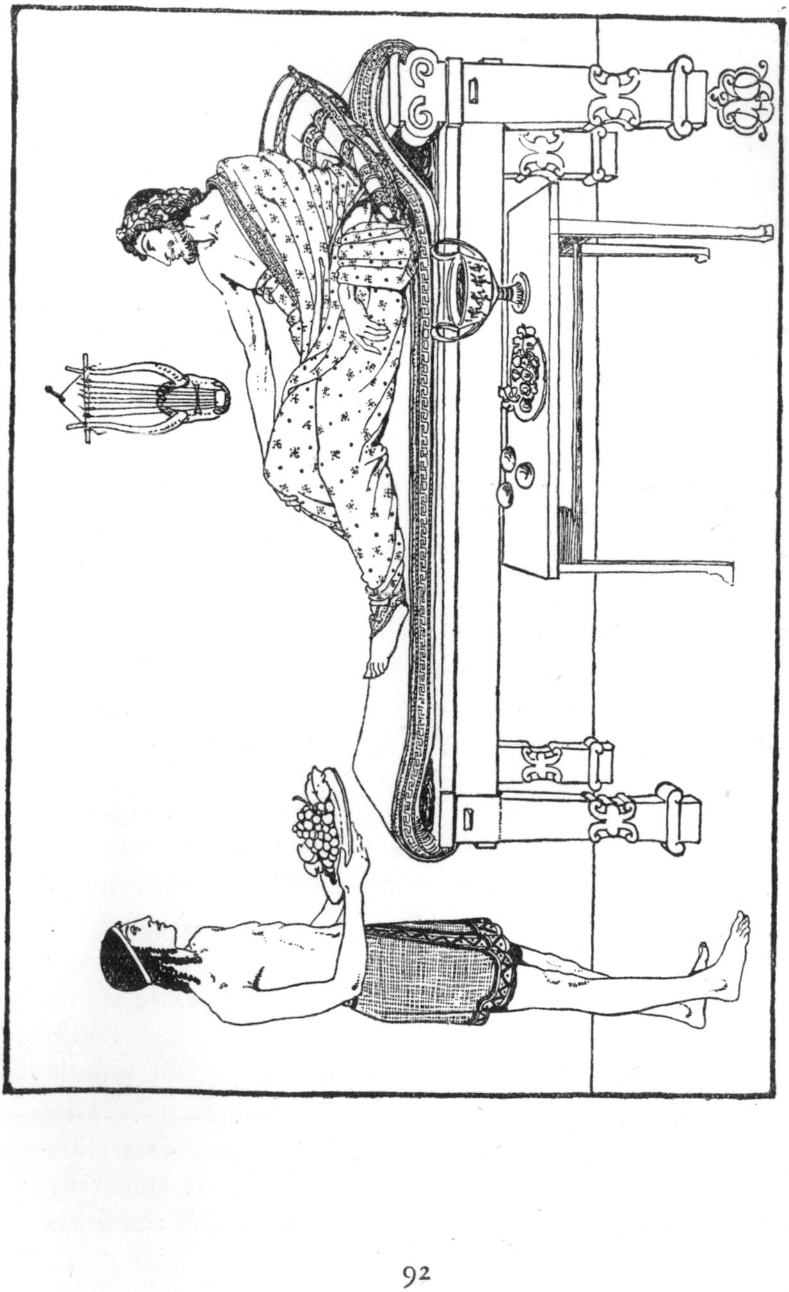

FIG. 53.—Couch and Table.

(Reconstructed from Black-figure Vase Drawings, British Museum.)

of a swan's head on the back, and the front and the back legs have been framed up so that the wider and more ornamental face came at the side of the chair. In Fig. 58 it comes in the front. In each case we have fol-

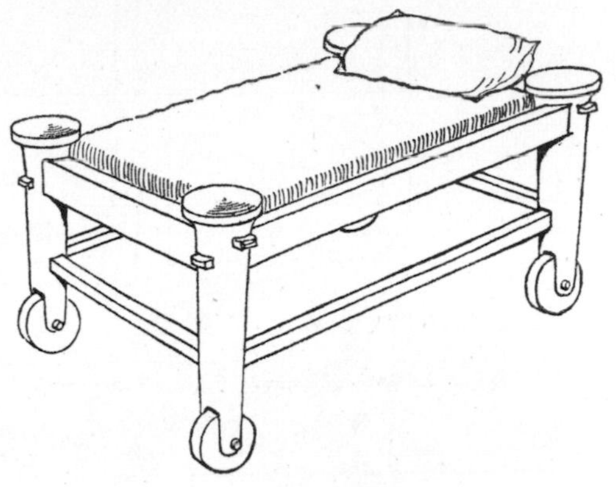

FIG. 54.—A Baby's Cot.

lowed the sculptors, but they may have put the pretty part where it suited the design. The actual seat of the chair was probably of leather thongs, to support the loose cushion which hung over a little in front and at the back. Fig. 56 has turned legs, and Fig. 57 claw-and-ball feet. This is not by any means the first appearance of this type of foot. Tutankhamen's throne had animals' feet.

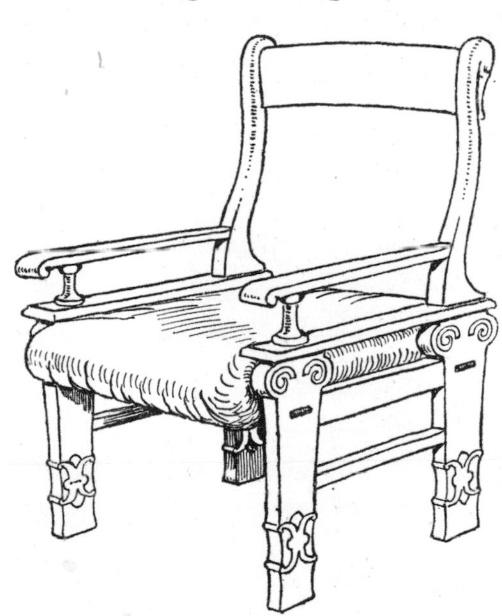

FIG. 55.—Chair from the Harpies' Tomb.
(*British Museum.*)

It should be noted that we did not add the tenons shown in our reconstruction. The sculptor, most obligingly, cut them in the original marble. The same thing occurs with the figures from Branchidæ in the

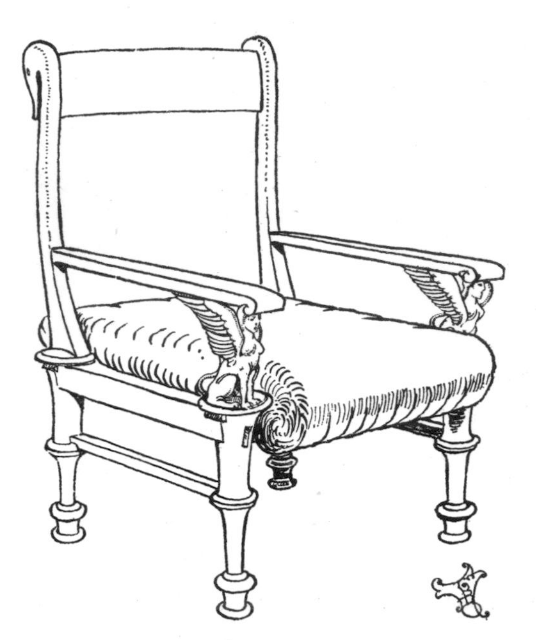

FIG. 56.—Chair from the Harpies' Tomb.

FIG. 57.—Chair from the Harpies' Tomb.
(*British Museum.*)

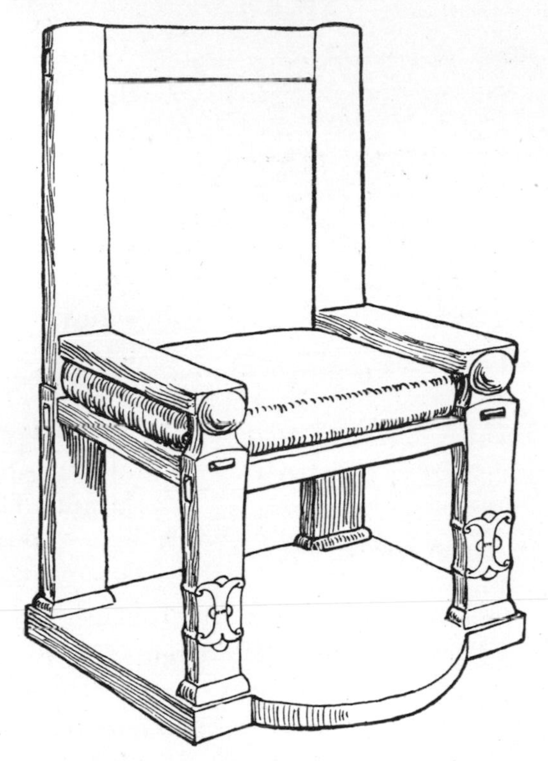

FIG. 58.—Chair of Figures from Branchidæ.
(*British Museum.*)

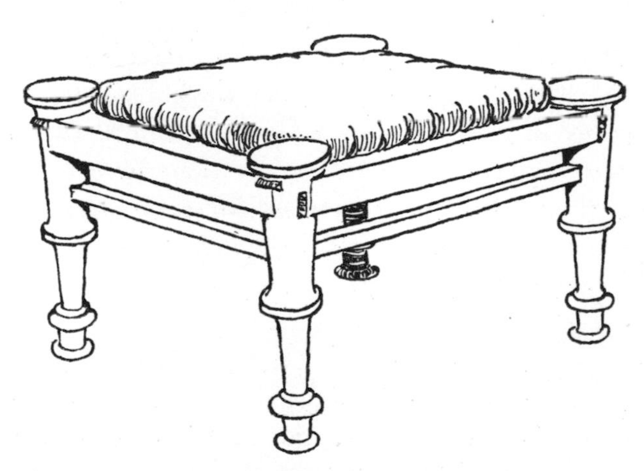

FIG. 59.—Stool.
(*Parthenon Frieze, British Museum.*)

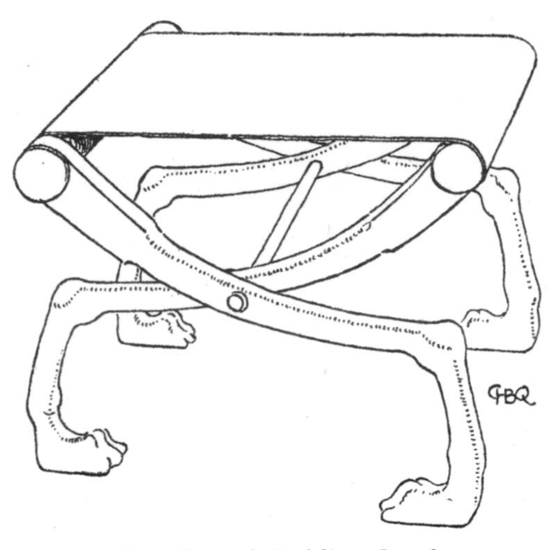

FIG. 60.—A Folding Stool.

Archaic room at the British Museum. These figures, seated on their thrones, and cut out of marble, once stood along a processional way leading to the Temple of Apollo at Didyma, near Miletus, in Asia Minor. Herodotus says that there was an oracle there from very ancient times which the Ionians and Æolians consulted. These figures date from 580 to 520 B.C. Fig. 58 shows one of the thrones.

Figs. 59 and 60 show stools. The next time you buy a sketching stool, you can remember its Greek prototype, and that even before this the Egyptians had thought of it.

The Greek women as well seem to have had all kinds of pretty little things, like wicker-work baskets, to keep their wools in; mirrors in which to admire themselves, and bronzes, like Fig. 26, to satisfy their love of beauty; pins for their hair, and brooches for their dresses. The very best place to study these is the Greek and Roman Life room at the British Museum.

EDUCATION

We may be sure that the Greek mother was not too much occupied with her housekeeping to find time to superintend the education of her children, and she could then, as now, send them to school. In the sixth book of Herodotus we are told that the roof of a schoolhouse had fallen in upon their boys (Chios), who were at lessons. This was about 494 B.C., and there were 120 pupils in the school. Herodotus seems to have mentioned the school, not as a rarity, but because of the tragic result of the roof falling and killing nearly all the pupils. We can take it, then, that there were schools in Greece in the Archaic period before Salamis. These would not, of course, have been schools as we understand them, with separate classrooms all furnished with forms and desks. We should not have found these in the sixteenth-century English school. Take Berkhamstead School, in Hertfordshire, founded by Dean Incent in 1541 ("E.T.," Vol. II.), as a very good example of a sixteenth-century grammar school, and we find that the accommodation, when it was founded, consisted simply of a hall, which was the schoolroom, and a house at each end, one for the master and the other for the usher. The Greek school at Chios could not have been much simpler than this.

The boys were sent to school when they were about seven, and went accompanied by an old slave, who appears to have gone inside with them, perhaps to help maintain order. On the vases, the boys are shown standing before their masters, who are seated on stools. This must be a convention, because there can hardly have been one master to each boy. On a red-figure vase one master plays a flute, another looks at a written exercise, the third master and pupil each have a lyre, and the fourth reads from a roll.

If we go to the Greek and Roman Life room at the British Museum we can see some of the actual apparatus of the Greek school. From this it is obvious that the pupils were well grounded in the three R's of reading, writing, and arithmetic. There is a terra-cotta group of an old schoolmaster, with the pupil standing at his side and reading from a roll. There are, as well, other exhibits of a Greek alphabet inscribed on marble, and a spelling exercise on a piece of pottery. Xenophon gives us an idea of what the boys read when he makes one of the characters in the " Symposium " say, " My father, anxious that I should become a good man, made me learn all the poems of Homer."

Writing was done on wax-coated tablets. These were made of wood, and the central panel was surrounded by a flat, raised edge, which served to protect the wax coating on the panel. Several tablets were strung together on strings, passed through holes bored in the edges. The writing was scratched on the wax surface with the sharp point of a stylus. At the British Museum there is a tablet which has a multiplication table and a reading exercise on it, and a beautiful ivory stylus found in a fifth-century B.C. tomb at Eretria in Eubœa. The stylus is very interesting, because the other end is flattened so that mistakes could be scratched out.

Paper made from Papyrus, and pens and ink, were used for important documents.

Now that we have arrived at arithmetic, we should like to join forces with the youngest of our readers, and examine this mystery hand-in-hand. We might all say together, as loudly as is possible in print, that we are not at all satisfied with the way this subject is taught, nor can we understand why so many boys have to be coached in Mathematics before they can pass the School Certificate.

There is a good tale told of a nice old man, who, during the war, helped in a school by teaching mathematics. He was doing a sum on the blackboard, and the sum took charge. It ran into millions, billions, trillions—it did everything but resolve itself into an obvious answer, and the master, taking a duster in his hand, said, " Well, boys, so far as I am concerned, this must remain a mystery"—and that is what the subject remains to many of us. There must be some reason for this, and we think one of the causes is that we have such excellent arithmetical symbols: 1, 2, 3, 4, 5, and so on, are so flexible, and can be added, subtracted, and multiplied with such ease, that they cease to be symbols, and become conjuring tricks instead; the answer comes out of the hat instead of the head under it.

Now let us see how the Greek boy did his arithmetic. He was handicapped by a most inadequate set of symbols. His numerals followed the alphabet, so he had letters instead of numbers. This was in reality a great help, because he was thrown back on his fingers to count with (hence, digit, a finger, for a number under 10), or pebbles (hence, calculate, from calculus, a pebble), or the abacus or reckoning-board. The abacus must have been a very useful implement. Here it is at A, in its simplest form of pips, or beads, on wires.

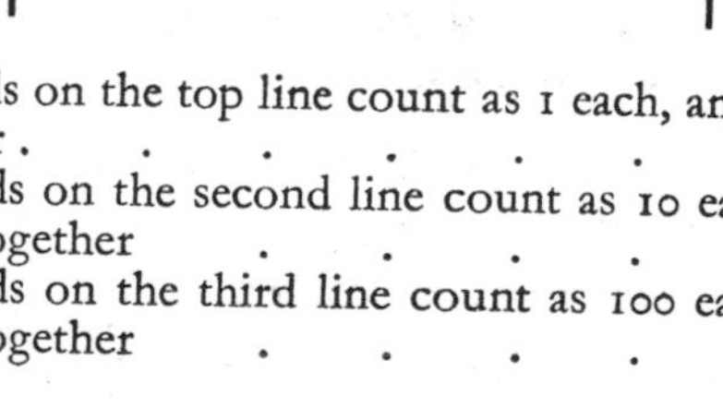

A

—OOOOOOOOOO—

—OOOOOOOOOO—

—OOOOOOOOOO—

The ten beads on the top line count as 1 each, and added together	= 10
The ten beads on the second line count as 10 each, and added together	= 100
The ten beads on the third line count as 100 each, and added together	= 1000
All the beads	= 1110

As to how the Greek boy used the abacus we cannot say; but even to people with non-mathematical minds like ourselves it is quite easy to see that addition would not be difficult to do.

B1	B2
—OOOO————OOOOOO—	—OOOOO————OOOOO—
—OOOOOOOOO————O—	—OOOOOOO————OOO—
—OOOOOOOO————OO—	—OOOOOOOO————OO—

Supposing you wished to add 216 and 15 and 4. The two 100's would be slipped to the right as B1, then one 10 and six 1's for the 16. Then comes 15. You want one 10 and five 1's, but you have only four 1's left. However, you can get over this by adding two more 10's to the right, and slipping back five 1's to the left, but you must return four of these to add the 4, and complete the addition. Your abacus, as B2, will then have two 100's at the bottom, three 10's above it, and five 1's, or a total of 235.

B2 will serve to illustrate subtraction. If you wished to subtract 235 from 1110, by moving these pips to the right you can read off that there will remain on the left eight 100's, seven 10's, and five 1's, or a total of 875. Unless our arithmetic is at fault, this is what remains when 235 is subtracted from 1110. Multiplication could have been turned into an addition.

It must be remembered that the abacus is still used in Russia and the Far East as a ready-reckoner. We saw one recently in the Anthropometrical Department of London University, in use by a Chinese student, Mr Tiang Liang Woo. This was of the same type as the one used by the Romans, with a dividing line. Starting on the right-hand side, the 5 beads under the line equals 1 each, and the two beads over the line equals 5 each. In this way the number of the beads is reduced, and the abacus kept smaller. It was very interesting to find this very ancient calculating machine in use side by side with the most modern types.

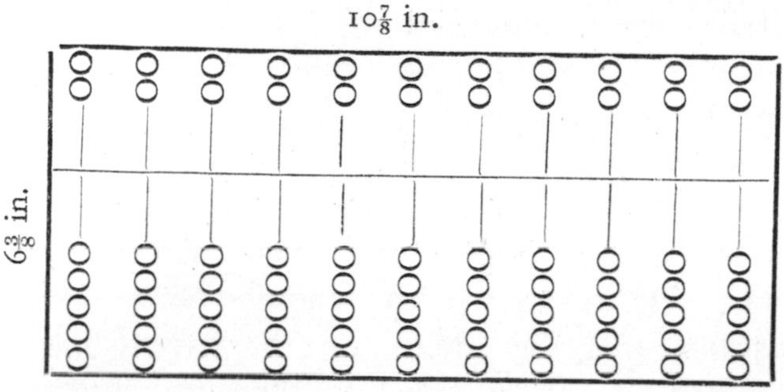

$10\frac{7}{8}$ in.

$6\frac{3}{8}$ in.

The great advantage of the abacus must have been that the Greek boy could experiment with numbers, and discover the difference between odd, even, and prime. He ceased to think of them as numbers, they came to life, became things, and he saw them. This is proved by the names he gave them. The root of a square number was called its side. The gnomon, originally the upright pointer of a sundial, was employed to indicate a square, which was shown arithmetically thus, 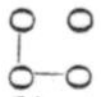 : the square root here was literally the side of the diagram. Or the Greek boy could build up a square of pips on his abacus, and find the square root quite simply.

In the same way, in geometry, the words used show that the Greeks saw these things: isosceles comes from Greek words for equal and leg; equilateral from equal-sided; parallelogram from contained by parallel lines; parallelepiped, from parallel and plane, and hypotenuse from to stretch under.

Thales of Miletus (624-546 B.C.) in Ionia, Asia Minor, was one of the first philosophers who was interested in arithmetic. He travelled in Egypt, and probably saw there the methods of the Egyptian land surveyors to which Herodotus referred in his Book II. (p. 13). The famous Rhind Papyrus in the British Museum (about

1700 B.C.) gives rules for measuring areas. The Egyptians knew that a triangle having its sides of lengths of 3, 4, and 5 is right-angled, and used this method of setting out right angles. Probably they did not know the proof, and this was left to Euclid (323-283 B.C.).

It is thought that Thales invented the theory of geometry. Pythagoras of Samos, like Thales, travelled, and was another philosopher who was interested in numbers. He is known to schoolboys by his famous proposition, that the square on the hypotenuse of any right-angled triangle is equal to the sum of the squares on the other two sides, and he probably did this by making models.

By the way, Greek schoolboys in the Archaic period were saved from algebra because this was not invented until the third century B.C., by Diophantes of Alexandria.

Our girl readers, by this time, may be wondering what happened in regard to the education of Greek girls—we are afraid, not very much. In Xenophon's "Œconomicus," to which we shall refer in the next volume, the young wife of Ischomachus had passed her girlhood "under the strictest restraint, in order that she might see as little, hear as little, and ask as few questions as possible."

Music

We can now consider music, and the great importance which the Greeks attached to it. Plato, later on, was to point out that education should have two divisions, gymnastic for the body, music for the soul—and music included literature, because poetry was chanted to the accompaniment of the lyre. That is why we talk of lyric poetry as being of the nature of a song, in which the poet tells us his thoughts. Epic poetry is a recited narrative of the doings of a hero perhaps, and dramatic poetry would be acted.

Plato said that music should be considered for its words,

melody, and rhythm. Certain harmonies he disliked very much. The Ionian and Lydian are instanced as being relaxed and soft, and more suitable for drinking parties than the education of the young. For this later purpose the Dorian and Phrygian harmonies were preferred, because these had a strain of courage and temperance. To-day we have disputations between the generation

FIG. 61.—The Music Lesson.

which, when it was young, before the war, swayed as it danced to the " Blue Danube " and its children who slide around to the latest jazz tune. Perhaps Plato summed up the whole matter when he said that " Beauty of style and harmony and grace and good rhythm depend on simplicity —I mean the true simplicity of a rightly and nobly ordered mind and character, not that other simplicity which is only an euphemism for folly."

Passing to instruments, he condemned the flute for its " composite use of harmony." The lyre and harp were allowed for use in the city, and pipes for shepherds in the country. We will consider the lyre first, and here we can turn to the Homeric Hymns, which, if not composed by the same hand as the " Iliad " and " Odyssey," are of great age. In the hymn, or lay, to Hermes, we find that it was the messenger of the gods to whom the Greeks credited the invention of the lyre. When young, he found a tortoise feeding on grass, and very unkindly choking the creature, scooped out its inside with a gouge of grey iron. He then "cut to measure stalks of reed, and fixed them in through holes bored in the stony shell of the tortoise, and cunningly stretched *round* it the hide of an ox, and put in the horns of the lyre, and to both he fitted the bridge, and stretched seven harmonious chords of sheep-gut."

Now for our reconstruction (Fig. 62). We should like to explain that the shell used was brought from Greece some years ago by a sailor-man; and we did not choke the creature, nor can we offer any suggestion how Hermes managed to do so, unless his tortoise kindly obliged by putting out his head. Fig. 62 shows the back, or carapace, of the tortoise, and what is more important, the belly, or plastron, and the fact that it is attached to the carapace. This seems to have been lost sight of by many writers, who assume that Hermes stretched the ox-hide across the belly, as if the lyre were like a banjo. The hymn is explicit, that the ox-hide was stretched round the shell, obviously with the idea of closing the holes in it fore and aft, used by the tortoise for projecting his head and legs. The stalks of reed may have been drilled across from edge to edge of these holes, as supports for the ox-hide, and to add to the resonance. When you hold the tortoise-shell in your hand, and tap the plastron, the sound is curiously like the noise made by the belly of a violin when tapped in the same way. Perhaps this gave Hermes his idea, and if it did, then the front of the violin started life as the bony belly of a tortoise.

There are in the Greek and Roman Life room at the British Museum the remains of an early lyre found in a tomb at Athens. The horns in this case are of sycamore, on to which the top bar is jointed, as shown in Fig. 62. This precluded tightening the strings by tuning, as with violin pegs, so it seems as if each string was pulled as

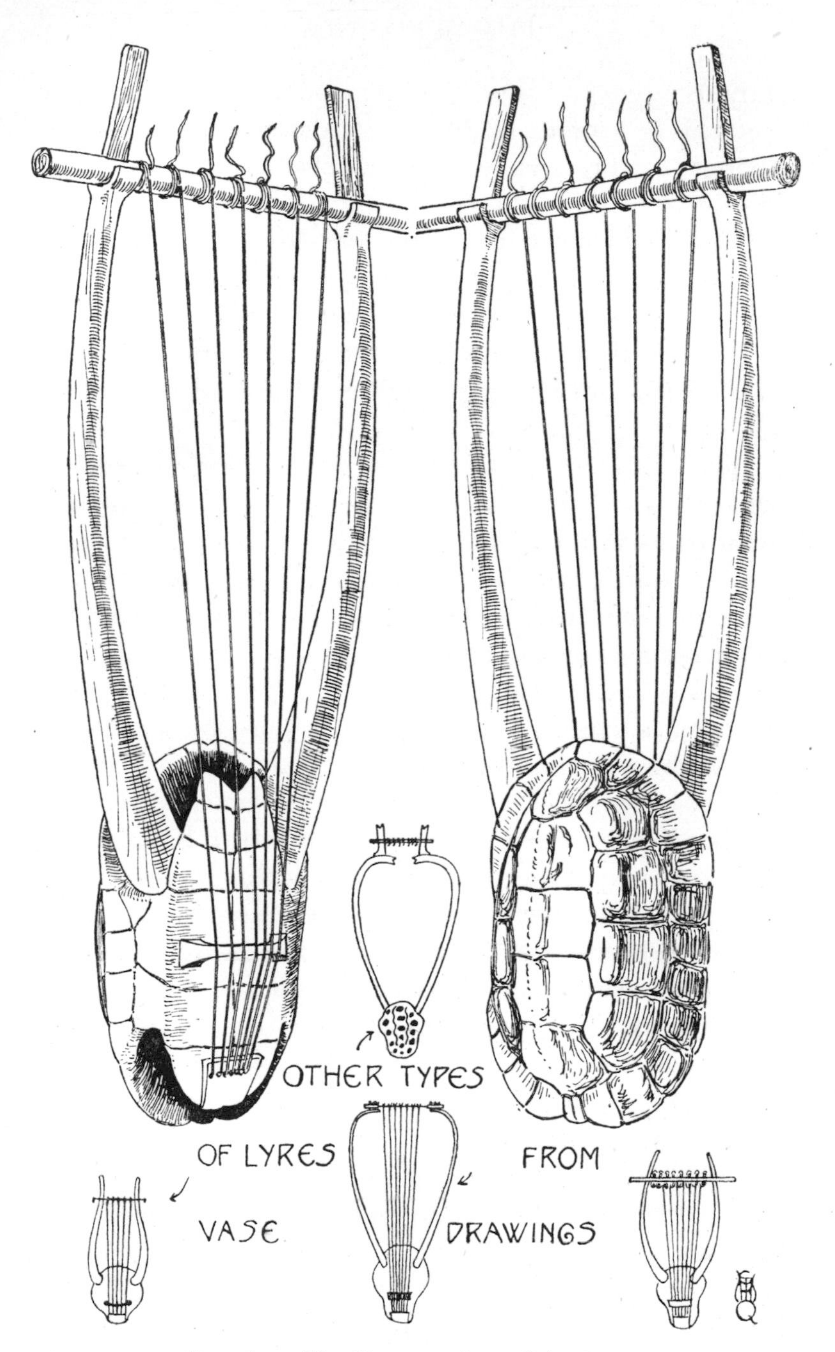

FIG. 62.—The Construction of the Lyre.

tightly as need be round the bar and then tied. This is suggested by some of the vase drawings. The small drawings in Fig. 62 are from black and red figure vases.

The kithara must have been developed from the lyre. It seems to have been the instrument used by professional musicians at public festivals, while the lyre was used in the home. It represents the same idea, but the body of the instrument was made of wood instead of tortoise-shell.

This leads us naturally to Pythagoras' interesting discovery, that the musical intervals correspond with certain ratios in the lengths of strings at the same tension. Thus the fourth, fifth, and octave of the note are produced by stopping the string at three-quarters, two-thirds, and half of its length. This can easily be tested on any fiddle. This is just one more example of the inquiring Greek spirit. One assumes that the Greek musicians must have had some scale before the time of Pythagoras, as primitive people of to-day have, but it was not a scientific one. Pythagoras of Samos lived 572-497 B.C. and, like our own King Alfred, was "curiously eager to investigate things unknown." He was a philosopher, mathematician, and geometrician, who hoped to find the key to beauty and harmony in some subtle combination of numbers. We must think of him as playing the lyre, and stopping off one of the strings at half of its length, and being struck by the quality of the note produced, and then going on until he had found the scientific solution. Trial first, then the proof was the Greek method.

Then there were pipes, which Plato thought the shepherds in his "Republic" could play in the country, and he seemed to think them safer than flutes. But the pipes were invented by Pan, who was the son of Hermes, and had goats' legs and horns, and whose friend was

Echo. One of the Homeric Hymns is dedicated to Pan :—

> "Tell me, Muse, concerning the dear son of Hermes, the goat-footed, the twy-horned, the lover of the din of revel, who haunts the wooded dells with dancing nymphs that tread the crest of the steep cliffs, calling upon Pan the pastoral God of the long wild hair."

Pan's pipe, or the syrinx, was made of graduated reeds, fastened together with wax and cords. He was the god of the country, and protected flocks, but wandered in the forests, and led dances of the nymphs. If you heard his pipes, then there was no saying what might happen. Echo would take up the refrain, and you be cast in panic fear. We met once an old peasant in Sicily playing on a pipe, and the tune he played was the jolliest little tune we have ever heard. It must have been invented long before Pythagoras invented his scale, and it rippled along, and went a little bit up, and a little bit down. We bought the pipe, but the tune eluded us, and now we think the peasant was not a peasant at all, but Pan himself.

Dancing

Notwithstanding Plato, the flute was the instrument the Greeks used to accompany dancing, and it was played in pairs, by the help of a mouth-band. The dancers often used castanets. Dancing with the Greeks had a religious character. A dance would be performed at a public festival in honour of a god or goddess. Women danced at home for their amusement, but not men and women together as with us. It is curious, but men and women seem to have been much better companions in the "Iliad" and "Odyssey" than they were in Archaic or Classical Greece. Perhaps this was because in between these times many of them had emigrated to Asia Minor and rubbed shoulders with Oriental peoples. Penelope had as good a time as the wives in the Viking Burnt Njal saga, to which we referred in "Everyday Life" in Anglo-Saxon and viking times. The Greek men do not seem to have danced. The tale of Hippoclides, on p. 24, shows that the guests were rather shocked at his performance. It was more usual for professional dancers to perform at the symposia or banquets. Judged by the vase drawings, Greek dancing consisted of a series of graceful rhythmic movements of the body and arms, assisted by the swing of the draperies.

There is a most beautiful drawing of girls dancing, on a vase shaped like a knuckle-bone, in the third Vase room at the British Museum. Any of our readers who are interested in drawing should make a point of seeing this. The tiny figures of the girls have an airy grace, and the drawing an exquisite delicacy, which inspires and yet depresses anyone who tries to use a pencil.

Games

Writing of knuckle-bones reminds us that this was a game played by women. Knuckle-bones came from the ankle joint of cloven-footed animals. The five small prettily shaped bones were thrown into the air, one at a time, and had to be caught and retained on the back of the hand. We have seen, on p. 9, how Herodotus gave the credit to the Lydians for inventing this game.

In the Metropolitan Museum in New York there is a terra-cotta group of two girls pickaback. This, apparently, was a kind of forfeit for failure in a ball game. In the same place there is a toilet-box with a drawing on it of two girls. One stands behind a wicket in exactly the same attitude as a wicket-keeper, and the other girl is throwing a ball in—the batsman or batswomen is absent, otherwise it looks exactly like an early game of cricket. Women are shown on another vase in New York whipping tops. In Vol. I., p. 58, we have seen how Nausica fell to playing ball. Hoops are often shown on the vases.

CHAPTER IV.—LIFE OUTSIDE THE HOUSE

It must always be borne in mind that though we think of the city state as being typical of Greek civilisation, the city was a very small one judged by modern standards. The people were not huddled together in a mass of houses, with the country miles away, and only to be reached by a long journey through dreary suburbs. The Acropolis at Athens was at one time the actual town, a city on high, with the country coming right up to its walls, and even in the time of Pericles it was a tiny little place.

Each city was the centre of a much larger agricultural district, so the Greek was very fortunately placed. He could civilise himself by living in the city and rubbing shoulders with his fellow-men in the market-place and gymnasia, or retire to the quietude of his farm in the country if he needed rest and peace.

We gave details in Vol. I. of eighth-century B.C. country life from Hesiod's "Works and Days," and in Vol. III. we shall use Xenophon's fourth-century "Œconomicus" for the same purpose. In the Archaic period the life of the Greek countryside was probably just as pleasant as that described by these authors.

Farming

One thing to be noted, however, is that Hesiod paints a picture of a life as laborious as that shown in "Joseph and his Brethren." Hesiod's eighth-century B.C. Greek farmer, and Freeman's East Anglian of the nineteenth century A.D., only wrest a living from the soil by labour as persistent as that of the French peasant of to-day. By the time Xenophon was writing, conditions had become much easier, and slaves were employed to do the hard work. Slavery seems to have started with the enslavement of the natives by the Dorians when they invaded Greece.

FIG. 63.—Treading Grapes.

The position of the slaves does not seem to have been worse than the English villeins of the Middle Ages. They were attached to the land, and had to work for their masters. As many of them were prisoners of war, they were not regarded as a race apart.

The black-figure vases frequently show country-life scenes. Men beat down the olives from the trees, and women pick them up, just as they do to-day, and ploughing is another subject.

Fig. 63 shows a vintage scene which has been reconstructed from a black-figure amphora illustrated in Busschor's "Greek Vase Painting." The grapes are being trodden out in a large wicker basket, mounted on a three-legged stool, with a spout to it to conduct the wine into a jug. In the original the work is being done by satyrs, who were attendants on Dionysus, the giver of wine.

The satyrs, and their female companions the mænads, are often shown on the vases, and, generally speaking, they are "full of beans"—sometimes too much so. They laugh, dance, skip, and indulge in the most irresponsible gambols, and their habits are not polite. However, this is probably an entirely wrong and twentieth-century point of view. Dionysus and his attendants represented, not so much wine and pleasure, as the life and fertility of vegetation.

The satyr is always shown with a tail like a horse and pointed ears—the mænads have no caudal appendage.

Demeter was the corn spirit. In one of the Homeric Hymns, we hear how she brought famine to the land. Persephone, the daughter of Demeter, was stolen by Hades, the god of the dead, for his wife, by Zeus' permission. Demeter, in revenge, prevented the growth of the crops until the gods gave her news of her daughter. Hermes, the messenger, was then sent to Hades, to tell him that he must send back Persephone to her mother,

FIG. 64.—Satyr with Wine Skin, *c.* 500 B.C.
(*British Museum.*)

but, before doing so, he gave her sweet pomegranate seed to eat. This is the food of the dead, and whoever eats it must return to Hades; and this was Persephone's fate—for two-thirds of the year she was free to live with her mother, but for the remaining third she had to go back and reign as Queen of the Shadows.

In this hymn we hear of a drink made of meal mixed with water, and flavoured with the tender herb of mint.

So much for the Greek as a farmer. His own simple needs were corn for his bread, olive oil instead of butter, and goat's milk to drink, or wine diluted with water. At a festival he could sacrifice a heifer or kid and eat their flesh. He grew beans and peas, and kept bees to provide honey for sweetening purposes.

It was when he wished to dispose of his surplus produce that he was confronted by the problem which turned him into a sailor. He was like our own vikings. The fertile plains in Greece, like those in Norway, are often cut off from one another by mountain ranges in between, so it was much easier for the farmer to load his produce into a boat, and hugging the shore, sail to the next township to barter his wine for pottery. In this way he early learned the usages of the sea, and by the Archaic period he was trading all round the Mediterranean, and learning the details of the craft which was to stand him in such good stead at Salamis. Herodotus tells us in his third book that " twice a year, wine is brought into Egypt from every part of Greece "—in earthen jars.

FIG. 65.—Athenian Fabric, End of Sixth Century B.C.: Dionysus.

SHIPS

We have seen in Vol. I. how the Greeks sailed in their ships to the Trojan War, and Hesiod's eighth-century farmer was quite prepared to go to sea. In Vol. I. we reconstructed, as Fig. 73, a boat from a vase in the first Vase room at the British Museum, which dates from about 800 B.C. This must have resembled the Gokstaad viking ship, which we illustrated as Fig. 44 in Vol. IV. of the " Everyday Life " books. This boat was still

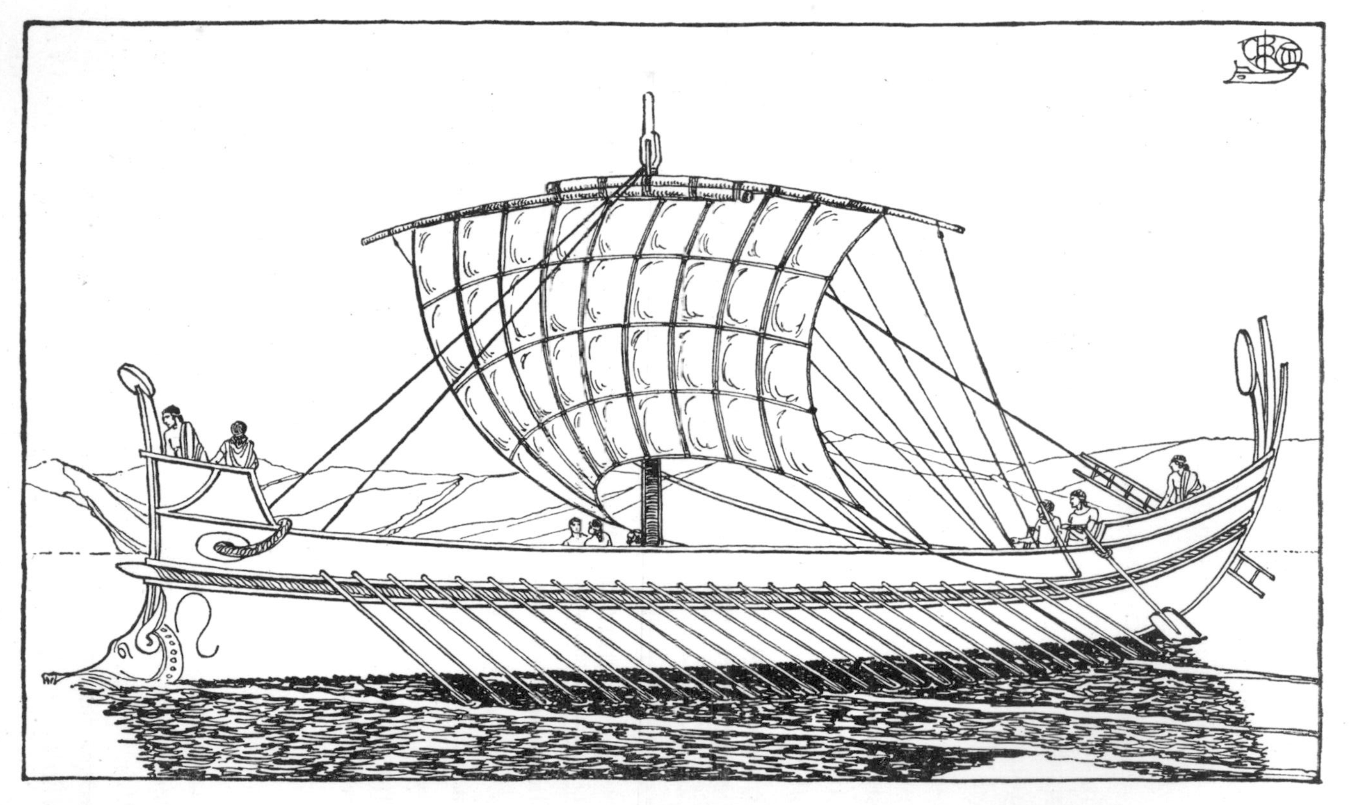

FIG. 66.—The Penteconter.

used in the Archaic period, and seems to have been referred to as a "long boat."

The next development seems to have been the penteconter, or fifty-oared galley. We have seen (p. 11) how Herodotus gives the credit for the first long voyages to the Phocæans of Asia Minor. He says they used the long penteconter, and not the round-built merchant ship, and that they explored the shores of the Mediterranean as far as Tartessus, near Cadiz. This was a very different business to sailing through the Cyclades to Asia Minor (see Fig. 2).

We have attempted a reconstruction of a penteconter in Fig. 66 from various vase drawings. It seems to have been the long boat, with a boar's head added as a ram and small decks fore and aft. In addition to the fifty oars, it carried one square sail—and here we come to an interesting problem, how this sail was reefed. If we refer to Fig. 42, it will be seen that horizontal lines run from the edge of the sail, and that in between these each section is bellied out—also that from the yard eight lines are shown coming down to the bulwarks.

From this it is thought that the sail, made of thin canvas, was divided up into squares, as shown in Fig. 66, by leather or webbing strips. On to the intersections of the strips a ring was sewn, and the bunt lines being passed through these, the sail could be triced up to give the steersman a better outlook forward, and reefed when it blew hard. On some vase drawings these bunt lines are shown coming from the foot of the sail. Mr R. Morton Nance came to our assistance in this matter, and he suggests that where the bunt line came from the yard, it may have been arranged as C, D, and F (Fig. 67), and from the foot of the sail as A, B, and E. It was really very much like the old-fashioned venetian blinds, made of thin laths of wood, which could be drawn up by cords. It remained

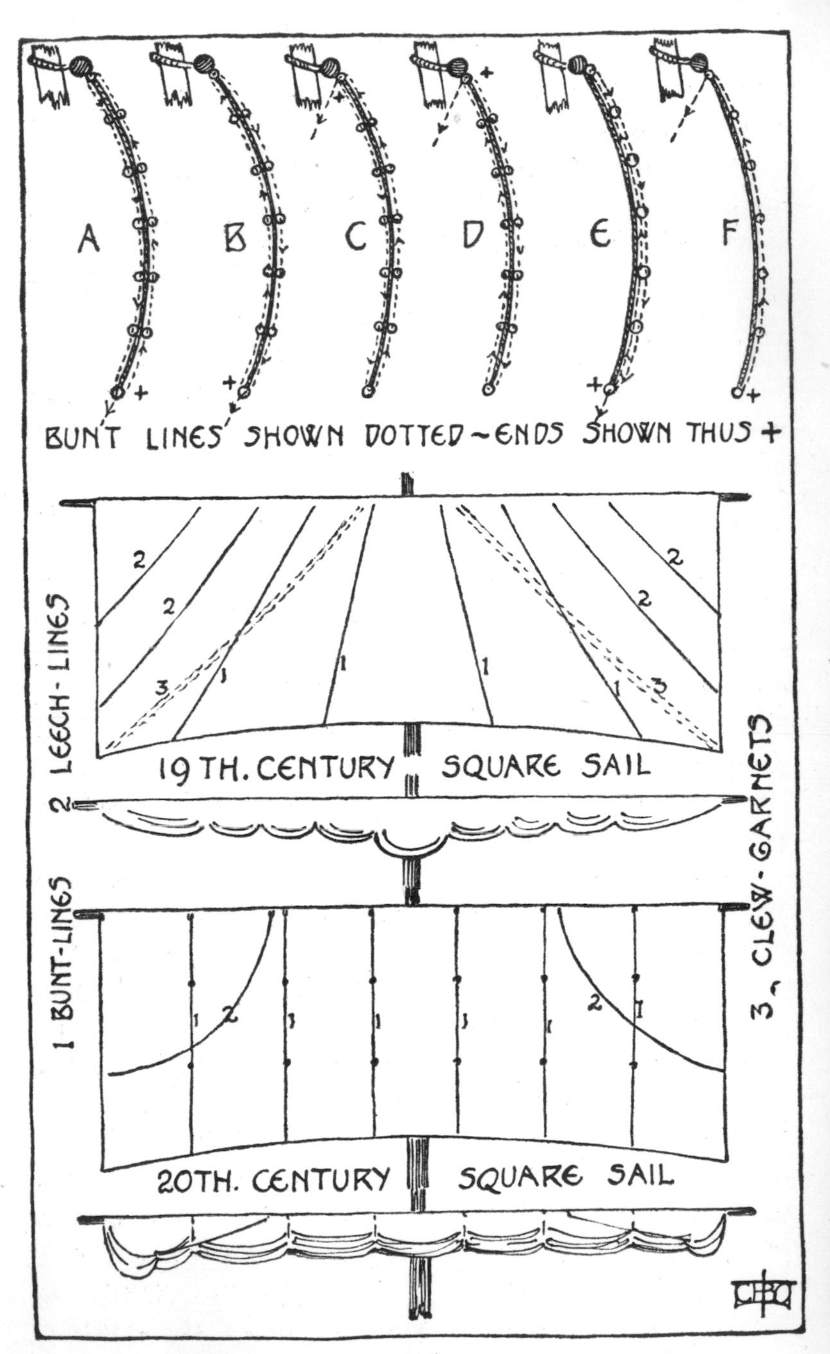

FIG. 67.—The Reefing of Square Sails.

on ships till Roman times, and we dealt with it in "The Ship of St Paul's Last Voyage," in "Everyday Life," Vol. III. Down-hauls may have been used to set the sail. It is rather interesting to note, in Fig. 67, how the bunt lines on twentieth-century square sails are arranged in a much more Greek way than those of the nineteenth century.

In addition, the penteconter, of course, had forestays and backstays to secure the mast, halliards to haul up the yards, sheets to secure the sail, and braces to pull round the yards.

Herodotus writes in the third book of an expedition of the Spartans against Samos, in the time of Cambyses, and says that this was the first time they went into Asia; also, that all ships in these early days were painted with vermilion. Think of a little fleet of penteconters sailing round a headland into a bay on the waters of which were the still reflections of surrounding mountains, and as the ships moved across the bay, each would have had its own red shadow—it must have been a goodly sight.

As to the round-built merchant ship, these are shown on the black-figure vases, and there is a good drawing on one in the shipping section in the Greek and Roman Life room at the British Museum. This we have reconstructed in Fig. 68. Obviously the hull is rounder, and not so long and snaky as the penteconter. It did not carry any oars, and depended solely on the one square sail. The rigging of this was much the same as the penteconter, and all this is very clearly shown. It is when we consider the superstructure of the hull that the trouble begins. Over the gunwale comes a long band of diagonal sloping lines, above this is another band of cross-hatching lattice, and above this again, supported on posts, a balustrade made up of three horizontal lines, with other vertical ones at intervals. Some writers have thought this was a ladder, but the ship is already provided with the one which was

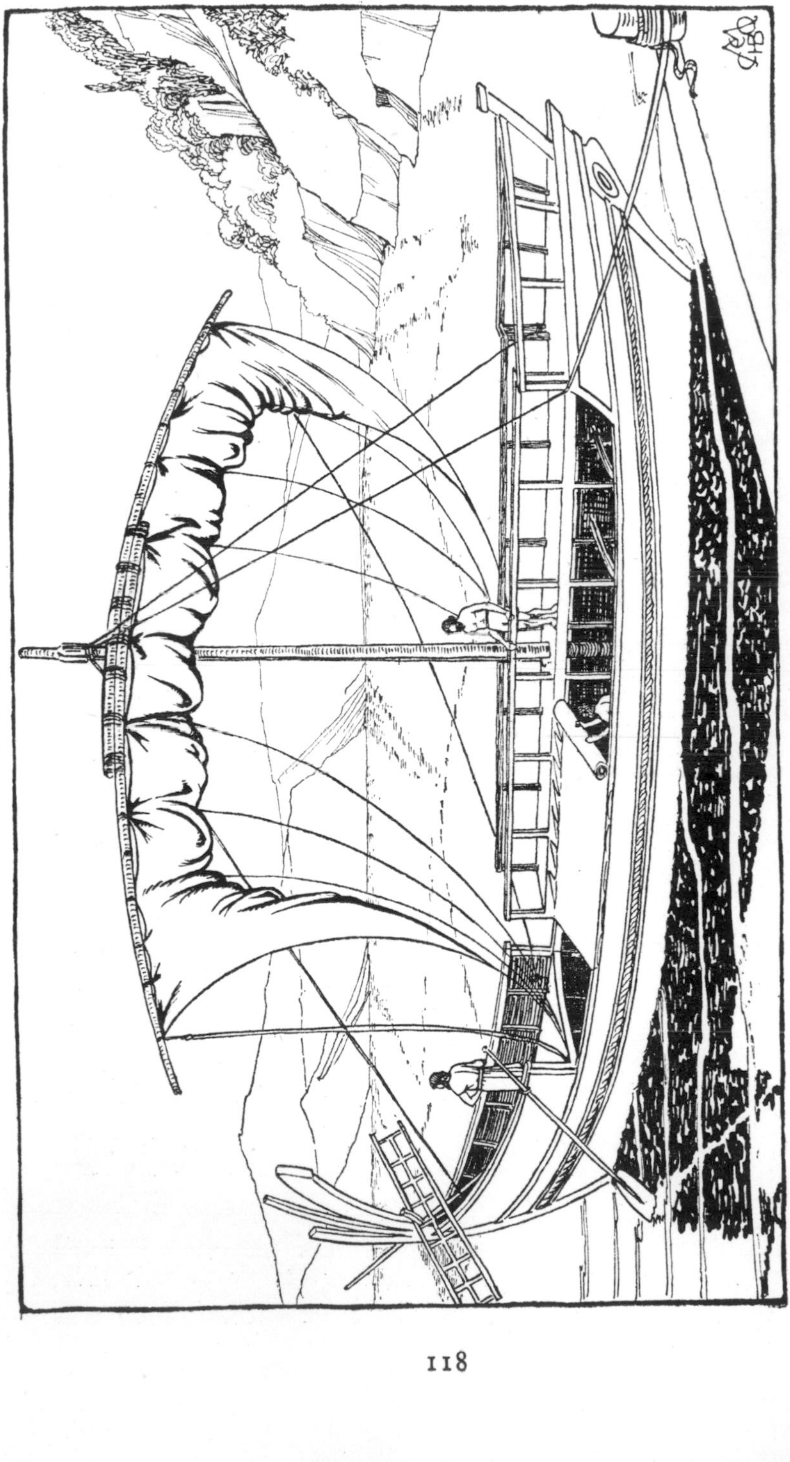

FIG. 68.—The Merchant Ship.

(From a Black-figure Vase at the British Museum.)

used for getting on or off, and shown in the usual place on the stern. Obviously there was no need for a second ladder, especially one nearly as long as the ship, so we take it that it really is a balustrade to a walk fore and aft, as shown on Fig. 68.

We assume that this was necessary, because the boat was not decked, and if this was the case, then the band of diagonal lines becomes a cloth which could be stretched along to protect the cargo, and the band of criss-cross is rope-lacing to secure the cloths.

Trade and Industry

All cargo boats, however, were not undecked. Fig. 69 shows a reconstruction of a very beautiful design on the inside of a black-figure Spartan drinking-cup (kylix) (Buschor, Plate XLVI.). It shows Arkesilas of Cyrene watching the loading of silphion into a merchant ship. Cyrene was a Greek settlement on the north coast of Africa (p. 17). That is why the old vase painter put in the monkey, just to show that he knew all about Africa. Herodotus, in Book IV., tells us that silphion (a carrot-like plant, 3 ft. high) was grown in North Africa, and used both for food and medicine.

In the design, we see how the silphion has been dried and baled up, and is being weighed before the king, and then, packed in sacks, is being taken down into the hold. The yard has been lowered, and swung inboard to support the scales, and the sail forms an awning for the working party. It is interesting to find that the balance-type of scale was used and not the steelyard of the Romans.

So far as industry is concerned, the building trade must have been in a prosperous condition in Archaic Greece. With all the temples to build, there could not have been much unemployment. Fig. 70 shows a carpenter using an adze.

Another important trade must have been that of the

Fig. 69.—The Loading of Silphion at Cyrene, Africa.

(From a Spartan Kylix.) Buschor, *Pl. XLVI.*

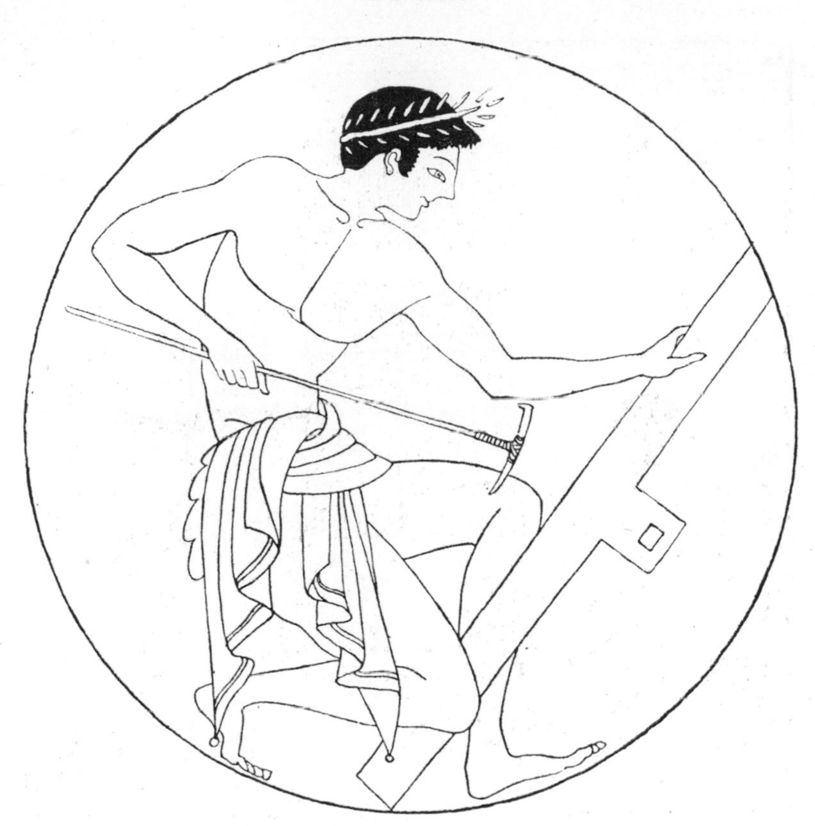

FIG. 70.—Carpenter with Adze, about 500 B.C.
Red-figure Goblet.
(*British Museum.*)

smith. How to provide himself with weapons or tools with a keen cutting edge, has always been a matter of prime importance to man. He first used flints, which he flaked to an edge, and we dealt with these in "Everyday Life in the Old and New Stone Ages." He then discovered bronze, and this metal was used in the Homeric period, which we described in Vol. I. Homer, writing the "Iliad" and "Odyssey," about the tenth century B.C., mentions iron, and it was about this time that it was taking the place of bronze in Greece.

As iron has been of so much use to man, it is worth

FIG. 71.—Iron Smelting.
(From a Black-figure Vase in the British Museum.)

while taking some trouble to find out how he smelted the ore. One of the earliest illustrations must be the drawing on the black-figure wine jug, in the second Vase room at the British Museum, which is Athenian ware of the end of the sixth century B.C. It is described there as showing the forge of Hephaistos, and we have reconstructed the drawing in Fig. 71. It is really a blast furnace, embodying the same design that is used to-day. A tower was built up, probably of bricks, with a lining of clay, and banded around to give greater strength. In the tower were placed layers of charcoal and ore, and a fire being

FIG. 72.—Ancient Iron Blast Furnace, near Gyalar in Hungary.
(From Model in Science Museum.)

kindled, the door in front was closed up, and a blast sent into the furnace from the bellows behind. This had the same effect that bellows have on an ordinary fire. The heat was maintained by closing the top of the furnace up. When the ore had melted, and the charcoal consumed itself, the metal slowly trickled down into a lump at the bottom of the furnace. This " bloom," as it was called, was reheated, and then forged into shape.

This type of furnace did not, of course, generate enough heat to make the iron run so that it could be cast. Bronze, however, melts at a much lower temperature, and there are vase drawings of foundries where bronze figures were cast from similar furnaces. We have dealt with various other methods of smelting employed by primitive people in Vol. II. of the " Everyday Life " Series.

Anyone who is interested in this most interesting subject, should pay a visit to the Metallurgical Section, XXIII., of the Science Museum in London. There they will find models of primitive open hearths used in Japan, and one of an ancient iron blast furnace discovered on a hillside at Gyalar in Hungary. We give a drawing (Fig. 72). It is such an interesting type that it would be worth while trying to reconstruct one in Sussex, say, where iron ore is found, and see if a " bloom " could be produced. Iron produced in this way is splendid for wrought-iron work.

CURRENCY

Money

Trade and industry lead us naturally to money. Unless the traders do their business by barter—or swopping, like some schoolboys—they need money as a medium for the exchange of goods. This is the only function of money, and the real basis of trade ; it also explains why money has sometimes taken such strange forms. We saw in "Everyday Life," Vol. II., how we used flat iron currency bars here in England in the early Iron Age before the Romans came. So long as these were recognised as currency, and not counterfeited, trade could go on.

Again, in small communities, where everybody knew everybody, it was usual to give credit to trustworthy people. The settlement took place after the harvest. They all totted up their tallies, and found out how they stood. The hard-working, far-seeing man might find that he was better off than the thriftless one. If some were one up, others were one down. However, a few currency bars or coins would enable them to settle their differences, and start all square again. But they had not made or lost money—they had made, or failed to make, goods.

There remains the question of price, which was, and still is, settled by supply and demand. If a majority of the Greek traders made wine, and only a few pottery, up went the price of the latter. The intelligent man would try to arrange his trading so that he could buy cheap and sell dear. If, however, a criminal began to buy up money, and gamble in currency, then he committed a crime against the community, because he restrained trade.

We saw, on p. 9, how Herodotus gave the credit to the Lydians for being the first people to use gold and silver coins. The Greeks adopted the money habit from the Lydians, and made their coins so beautifully that all the later coinages have been modelled on them. You can see them at the British Museum with the early gold staters of Crœsus.

COMMUNICATIONS

Travel

When the old Greek wished to travel on the land he used the chariot, and if he was anything like the modern Greek with a car, he must have been something like Jehu. However, the chariot must have suited his style of driving very well, and the rough tracks he had to go over. In the fourth book of the "Odyssey" there is a fine description of the chariot drive of Telemachus from Pylos to Sparta.

A fine Corinthian krater (Fig. 66 in Buschor) shows the departure of Amphiaros, who was one of the heroes of Argos. He was persuaded by his wife Eriphyle, who had been bribed by a necklace, to join in an expedition against Thebes, in which he knew he would be killed; so on setting out, he told his sons to punish their mother for his death. Not a very cheerful subject for the vase painter one would think, but he has drawn it just at the warrior's departure, and the only evidence of guilt is that the wife holds the fatal necklace in her hand. Just such a scene must have been seen in old Greece when any soldier went off to the wars, or the father of a family left on business travel. We have attempted a reconstruction in Fig. 1.

The chariot has been brought out of the entry, and the horses have been yoked to it. We described the chariot in detail on p. 116 of Vol. I. A groom stands at the horses' heads, a stirrup-cup is being handed to the charioteer, and he is shown on the vase, clothed in a long tunic, like the Delphic charioteer (Fig. 28). This, after all, was the equivalent of an overcoat, and a more comfortable driving garment than the shorter tunic. The family all stand round, and a little dog jumps up to say good-bye to his master. Lizards run up the wall; there is a scorpion, and what looks like a hedgehog—a most wonderful little picture.

By the way, it must be remembered that though, as

FIG. 73.—A Cart.
(*Black-figure Vase, British Museum.*)

we saw in Vol. I., the chariot was used in warfare in earlier times, by the Archaic period this had ceased to be the case.

The Greeks were good horsemen, and there are many fine vase drawings of them as such. Another mode of conveyance was a small two-wheeled cart, as Fig. 73, drawn from a black-figure vase.

Games

When we come to the amusements of men, the first place must be given to their organised games. These date from a very remote antiquity. The Greeks thought that they were originated by Heracles himself. In Vol. I. we noted how, in the twenty-third book of the "Iliad," Homer describes the games held after the funeral of Patroklos. Chariot racing, boxing, wrestling, and running were included.

Again, in this book, on p. 12, we saw how the dead Phocæans were honoured with "solemn games both gymnic and equestrian." This does not mean that all the games were always solemn, or only associated with funerals. In the sixth book of the "Odyssey" (see Vol. I.) we are told how the Phæacians entertained Odysseus. There was a sacrifice, then a feast, followed by games of running, wrestling, boxing, dancing, and casting a great stone. Like every other Greek doing, the games were held under the patronage of the gods, and after sacrifice had been made to them. Fundamentally, the games kept men fit and prepared them for war, as well they satisfied the Greek ideal—that a healthy body was necessary for a well-balanced mind. The Greeks, being artists, must have derived great pleasure from watching beautifully proportioned bodies in action.

It must have been at the games that the sculptors gained their inspiration, and saw the models which they translated into terms of beauty in marble. This was possible, because in the early days and the best periods there was no trace of professionalism, or the specialist, and the Pentathlon was introduced as early as 708 B.C. This consisted of five events—running, jumping, discus and javelin throwing, and wrestling. The prize, only a crown of wild olive, was given to the best all-round man; brain had to be added to brawn, and beauty to both. If the Greek athlete was anything like the men shown in the Parthenon frieze, then the Pentathlon, given suitable raw material, must have been the most scientifically designed course of physical culture the world has ever seen.

All over Greece we may be sure that every boy practised these five parts of the Pentathlon, hoping that he one day would be able to represent his city at Olympia. This great festival was first held in 776 B.C., and then every four years until A.D. 393.

Now we come to another useful purpose which the games served in Archaic Greece—they helped to keep the peace. We have seen that the people were quarrelsome. The small city States, which fostered genius, bred a strong local patriotism, which expressed itself in fierce intercity jealousies. Sparta and Athens were generally at loggerheads, and their dissensions are bound up in, and almost constitute, the history of Greece. Just as our own William the Conqueror introduced a Truce of God to stay his turbulent barons from killing one another ("Everyday Life," IV.), so the authorities at Olympia, every four years, sent heralds, wearing crowns of olive, to all the Greek States to proclaim a Truce of Sport. So for a time all the Greeks forgot their quarrels and engaged in friendly contests.

In the evenings, after the games, the people could talk to one another. We do not realise to-day how necessary talk was to the Greeks. There was no wireless, or newspapers, or printed books, so people had excellent memories, and the news was passed from one to another by word of mouth. We can be quite sure at one fifth-century Olympiad the history of one Herodotus, an Ionian, was discussed by his fellow-Greeks.

They came from all over the Greek world, and camped on the plain. Here there would have been a veritable town of tents, with stalls for food, and camp fires—rather like a fair in the Middle Ages, or a great rally of the Scouts to-day. Competitors arrived at Olympia some while before the festival, and went into training—as well, they had to satisfy the judges that they were of Greek birth.

The festival lasted for five days. All the competitors sacrificed to the gods, and swore that they had been properly trained, and would not cheat in the contests. The games opened with chariot and horse races, and then followed the Pentathlon.

Before we describe the games we had better set the scene of Olympia.

Its position on the map is shown in Fig. 2. The sacred enclosure was situated on level land at the foot of the Hill of Cronus at the junction of the Rivers Cladeus and Alpheus. The enclosure was called the Altis. On the north side was the temple to Hera, to which we referred on p. 38. This dates from about 700 B.C., and there were two earlier ones on the same site. The great Temple of Zeus, the ruins of which are now on the south side of the Altis, was not built until the fifth century B.C., nor, in all probability, the treasuries of the various Greek cities which formed the headquarters of the deputations sent to Olympia. In Archaic times all would have been much simpler: the temple set in an enclosure—an altar for sacrifice—simple buildings for treasuries—pleasant gardens and colonnaded walks, with statues set up to celebrated athletes. The stadium was to the east of the Altis, with earth banks for the spectators to sit on. The elaborate stone seats found at some places were added at later times.

FIG. 74.—Heracles, Sixth-Century Black-figure Vase.

The stadium was so named because its length was 1 stadion, or about 606 English ft., and its width about 30 yds., not quite so long as an English furlong of 10 chs. or 660 ft. Heracles is supposed to have stepped it out. The competitors raced up and down, and did not run round as we do. The track was covered with white sand. At Olympia you can still see the starting and finishing lines of the fourth century B.C. These were formed by letting stone slabs, about 18 in. wide, into the ground right across the course. In these, parallel grooves are cut about 7 in. apart, which appear as if they had been used by the runners to get a toe grip. We tried them, but they did not seem to be useful for a modern start. Again, at 4-ft. intervals, there are square sockets which must have taken wooden posts. The posts suggest that lines were stretched along the course. These would have been very useful for the short race of one length of the stadium. In longer races the posts alone would have served to fix the turning-points, because the Greeks had long-distance races of 7, 12, 20, and 24 stades.

Herodotus gives us an idea that, notwithstanding his oath, the Greek athlete wanted watching.

FIG. 75.—The Foot Race.

In the eighth book, Adeimantus says: "Themistocles, at the games they who start too soon are scourged." "True," rejoined the other, "but they who wait too late are not crowned." This explains why, on all the vase drawings, the referee, instead of being provided with a whistle, is always armed with a good strong rod.

We can now discuss the Pentathlon.

Jumping.—Greek jumping was a running long jump, as ours, except that the jumper was assisted by weights, which he held in his hands, and swung forward to assist him in his flight through the air. The weights weighed about $2\frac{1}{4}$ lbs., and the jump was made on the forward swing of the arms. The jumping-ground was dug up, and the jumps marked by little pegs. On a red-figure vase at the British Museum, a flute player is playing, and the jumper may have regulated the swing of his weights by the music. Apparently the Greeks did not have high jumps.

Throwing the Discus.—We read in Part I. how Odysseus threw a great stone, at the Phæacian Games, and at the funeral games of Patroklos, in the "Iliad," Polypoites flung a pig of iron "as far as a herdsman flingeth his staff." By Archaic times this had been regularised into a circular metal plate, from 6 to 11 in. in diameter, and weighing from 3 to 9 lbs. The thrower stood on a space marked off by lines in the front and at the sides, and his endeavour was to throw the discus as far as possible, not, as in quoits, to hit a mark. The discus was held above the head, the left hand holding the lower edge and the right hand the upper edge; it was then swung down in the right hand, and back again on the forward swing, to be thrown with all the weight of the body behind it. Our drawing (Fig. 77) has been drawn from Myron's "Diskobolus" (484-440), where the discus has been swung back, and is just going forward again. The record throw in the modern Olympic Games equals 160 ft.

Fig. 76.—The Long Jump.

FIG. 77.—Throwing the Discus.

Throwing the Javelin.—In " Everyday Life in the Old Stone Age " we collected some interesting details on throwing spears or javelins. The Tasmanians used one nearly 12 ft. long, made of hard wood ; its heavy-pointed end killed game at 40 to 50 yds., and they did not use a throwing-stick. The Australian aborigines used a spear, 10 ft. long, and a spear-thrower—this was a stick about 1 yd. long, with a handle at one end and a peg at the other. The peg fitted into a notch at the end of the spear, and as this was thrown, the thrower was kept in the hand, and helped to give the spear a final impetus.

The Greek javelin was about the height of a man, and was thrown by the assistance of a leather thong (the amentum) bound to the centre of the shaft, and into which the first two fingers were put. If the amentum was slightly twisted on the javelin, a rotary movement was given to it.

Xenophon, in his work on Horsemanship, writes of javelins of corneil wood, thrown from horseback. The rider advances his left side, and draws back his right, and rising on his thighs, launches the weapon with the point directed a little upwards.

Wrestling.—Wrestling is one of the oldest sports. With the Greeks a fall on any part of the body counted. If both wrestlers fell there was no count. Three falls gained the victory, and tripping was allowed. In our drawing (Fig. 79), which has been founded on a vase drawing, one man has played a clever trick on his opponent. He has seized his arm, turned, pulled him on to his back, and then pitched him over it.

Boxing.—Boxing is described by Homer in the funeral games of Patroklos, and in Vol. I. we wrote of the fight between Polydeuces, the champion of the Argonauts, and King Amycus. Greek boxing-gloves, until the end of the fifth century, consisted of thongs of ox-hide bound

Fig. 78.—Throwing the Javelin.

Fig. 79.—Wrestling.

FIG. 80.—The Pankration.

round the hands. Apparently there was not any ring, or rounds, or body-blows, or classes. They aimed at each other's figure-heads. Though the heavy-weight might score in the boxing, he would not have had any chance of winning the Pentathlon.

The Pankration.—This extraordinary event was first instituted in 648 B.C., and somehow or other it does not seem at all Greek. The pankration was a regularised rough-and-tumble fight to the finish. Wrestling, strangling, arm-twisting, hitting, kicking, and jumping on your opponent were allowed. Apparently you could do every-

FIG. 81.—Cock-fight: Corinthian Ware, Sixth Century B.C.

thing with, or to him, except bite him, or gouge out his eyes. It was drawn on the vases, and may have been rather comic in reality.

Sport.—Apart from the regularised games, there would have been other sports. Fig. 81 shows a cock-fight, which is an example of an unpleasant subject treated in a delightful way.

Hunting, of course, would have been indulged in, not so much as a pastime, but as a means of stocking the larder. Figs. 82 and 83 are animated little pictures from black-figure vases.

Having dealt with Life and Work, we come to Death and Funeral monuments.

Fig. 84 is a reconstruction of the Harpies' Tomb, from Xanthos, Lycia, in Asia Minor. The sculptured panels which formed the actual sides of the sepulchral chamber are now in the Archaic room at the British Museum. Originally this

FIG. 82.—Huntsman with Fox and Hare: Kylix (Goblet), about 520 B.C.

FIG. 83.—Olpe (Ware Jug): Attic Corinthian Fabric, Sixth Century B.C.

chamber was set up on the top of a tall shaft, as shown in our drawing. There was a small door into this chamber on the west side, closed by a slab of stone.

Its name was given when it was thought that the figures in the frieze were harpies carrying off the dead.

Now it is thought that the winged figures in the frieze show the Genius of Death carrying away, in a kindly fashion, the soul of the deceased person—the soul being shown by a miniature figure.

Fig. 85 gives the detail of one of the panels.

And now, having come to the end of our space—but not by any means the end of our subject—we must take leave of our readers for a little while. Meanwhile, we hope they will continue their own studies of Archaic Greece. If, after having read our book, they have got an outline in their minds, they can fill in the details by studying the black-figure vases in the second Vase room at the British Museum, and the sculptures in the Archaic gallery.

FIG. 84.—The Harpies' Tomb, from Xanthos, Lycia, Asia Minor.
(Archaic Room, British Museum.)

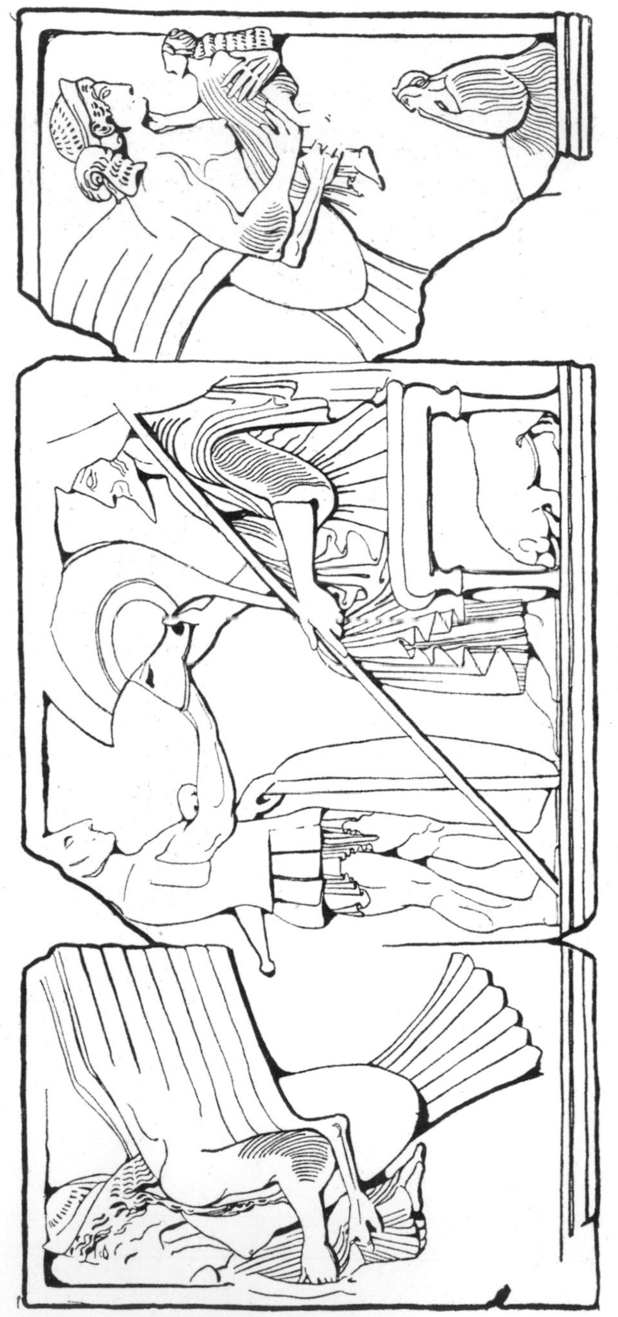

Fig. 85.—Harpies' Tomb, Xanthos.

INDEX

Note.—The figures in heavier type are illustrations.

Long vowels, as Fāte, Mē, Pīne, Nōte.

Short vowels, as Făt, Mĕt, Pĭn, Nŏt.

E always pronounced Œ and Æ, as *ee* in free, *eu* as feud, *c* as cane, *ch* as k.

A

B

C

INDEX

INDEX

T

U

V

W

X

Z

Printed in Great Britain at THE DARIEN PRESS, *Edinburgh.*